Scots Baror

Mansions & Castle Restorations
in the West of Scotland

MICHAEL C. DAVIS

Largie Castle.

SPINDRIFT PUBLISHING, SPINDRIFT,
ARDRISHAIG, ARGYLL, PA30 8EP
1996

Introduction

It may perhaps seem a little eccentric to write an essay describing not the original but the revived "baronial" style of Scotland, and then to restrict treatment of that revival to examples from the West of Scotland! There are, however, very good reasons for this beyond mere academic pedantry or the justification provided by a "local studies" approach.

The revival of Scots Baronial architectural forms and detailing has encompassed a wide variety of approaches, exploring virtually every romantic architectural response to the past from brutal adaptation, through nostalgic evocation, down to the self-effacing zeal of many modern castle restorers.

The decision to examine the West Coast and, in particular (but not exclusively) Argyll, is scarcely wayward. The *Gothick* Baronial of the 18th and early 19th centuries began on the shores of Loch Fyne at Inveraray. A few miles up the loch from Inveraray stands Dunderave, Robert Lorimer's most famous restoration. From Dunderave, one can see Ardkinglas, Lorimer's most successful Scots Revival mansion. In fact, Lorimer's two other great baronial mansions - Formakin and Rowallan - are found in the West, in Renfrewshire and Ayrshire respectively, while Craigends, one of the most spectacular of David Bryce's designs, now demolished, was built in Renfrewshire. So also, if the Baronial Revival as a whole may be considered to have begun at Inveraray, the later antediluvian traditions of certain of the Campbell (and other) gentry led to a series of "antiquarian" inclined houses built in Argyll from the 1840s, unique in their collective significance. These were echoed in the late 19th and early 20th centuries by an equally astonishing grouping of castle restorations, often undertaken at considerable expense with ancestral motives, or hobby -enthusiasms, in mind. In addition to these, there are many more mainstream examples of Scots Baronial. While it would be difficult today to write about late-Victorian or Edwardian Scots Baronial without some degree of reference to the work of Charles Rennie Mackintosh, now the most celebrated of the distinguished Glasgow architects of that time, the charming and appealing "Old Scots" work of William Leiper, also almost exclusively found in the West of Scotland, is probably of greater relevance to this essay.

In an attempt to avoid dispute over semantics, a few definitions are required. The "West of Scotland" or the "West Coast" is not intended to include the far North West or the South West of Scotland. It may be taken to run from South Ayrshire to Wester Ross, and inland to include part of Stirlingshire and Lanarkshire. "Scots Baronial" as a term has been used as consistently as possible; "Scottish Baronial" or even the 19th century "Scotch Baronial" might have been equally appropriate.

To speak of the Scots Baronial "Revival" may suggest (to the unwary) an agenda of common objectives or even the intention to reproduce past architecture. In fact, architects and their clients tended to adopt a variety of individual approaches to pillaging the past for a suitable idiom with which to clothe their contemporary objectives. As long as this *caveat* is borne in mind, "revival" remains a useful term with which to describe collectively a number of differing approaches, all of which have borrowed some degree of inspiration and romantic character from the architecture of the past.

The term "Scots Baronial" is, of course, now rightly accepted as a misnomer when applied to most original Scottish castles, in that their "baronialism" was symbolic rather than actual since they were generally tall, fortified houses built by prosperous lairds rather than military castles built by feudal magnates. As applied to the architecture of the Revival, it remains current, sanctioned by long usage and coloured by connotations of "balmorality" and the tartanry of taste. However, more specific terms such as "Old Scots" may be used to describe more sensitive interpretations. The term "castle restoration" is used in this essay in its more catholic sense and the controversy over the use of this term is described in the text.

The word "castle" has been used for many years to describe the original tradition of "mock military" fortified houses of lairds and the vertical palaces of aristocrats alike, and its meaning in a Scottish context is well understood. This usage is continued in this essay.

Finally, it is worth adding that this is essentially an architectural rather than a social history and, although it is undesirable to separate the two completely, social or political morality is not really an issue which is considered.

Acknowledgements

The idea of writing this book was formed in my teens, but was not carried into effect until after the 1993 Architectural Heritage Society of Scotland conference, "Scots Baronial". This piece therefore has its origins in my own paper, given then, but consideration of a number of issues was influenced by the contributions of Gavin Stamp, Frank Walker, Alistair Rowan, Ian Gow and Crichton Wood.

I must also thank a number of extremely helpful people, not least Murdo MacDonald, Argyll & Bute District Archivist. The staff of the excellent National Monuments Record of Scotland - in particular Ian Gow, Jane Thomas, Veronica Steele and Ruth Wimberley - have assisted with various enquiries, and Graham Ritchie kindly arranged permission to print a number of photographs belonging to the Royal Commission on the Ancient and Historical Monuments of Scotland. Individual owners of photographs and illustrations have also been most helpful.

Lastly, David Walker, Charles McKean, Marion Campbell of Kilberry, Andrew Duncan Jones, my wife Liz Davidson, and my parents, Chris and Elinor Davis, are all due my thanks for undertaking the tedious task of reading through my text in detail for errors of fact and grammar. I have not adopted all of their suggestions, so I need hardly add that the quirks of expression and the deficiencies of argument which remain are mine, not theirs.

Formakin - mansion.

Formakin - entrance to forecourt (Robert MacCallum).

Formakin - the miller's house.

Damned lie!

If, to many, the work of Robert Lorimer still represents the climax of the Scottish Baronial Revival, then his work at Formakin in Renfrewshire (which he hoped would be the purest thing in "Scotch" style he had ever done) forms a major part of this reputation, for good or for ill. Designed in the years before the Great War, Formakin is a large mansion, never finished internally, which wrestles with the key problem of squaring the planning of a 20th century mansion with something of the qualities, not least of massing, of an old Scots fortified house or "castle" of, in this case, 17th century date. Lorimer evidently valued the design, for he trotted out virtually the same drawings in a vain attempt to enthuse Sir William Burrell into building something very much like Formakin at Hutton Castle in Berwickshire.

Powerful image though the Formakin mansion may be (set amid a still unspoilt landscape), it is in fact the other buildings in the grounds which set the tone and turn its setting into a dream-like evocation of 17th century Scotland. Even the workers' "bothy" is an "old" towerhouse, the piggery is crowstepped, and the old mill and the miller's house bear exquisitely modelled features added by Lorimer. It would not be exaggerating to say that Formakin Estate is a baronial Brigadoon in impeccable taste, curiously similar in feel to the Auld Toon at the 1911 Glasgow Exhibition. The bothy, indeed, conspicuously wears a fictitious datestone of 1605, and the date "1695 D.L." appears over the entrance to the stable-yard. "D.L.", it would seem, stands for "Damned Lie...."

Sir John Stirling-Maxwell, writing in 1937, enthused that Lorimer's houses "are so completely saturated with the spirit of the old builders, and show so complete a mastery of their technique, that those who come unexpectedly upon them for the first time, as one may do at Formakin in Renfrewshire, are for the moment completely staggered, and where all is new, are left wondering how much is old".[1]

Even more tellingly, Stirling-Maxwell scorned the earlier generation of revivalist architects, such as William Burn and David Bryce, for building "unscholarly imitations of the old".[2] His emphasis of discontent most surely rests upon "unscholarly".

The implication of the stance of so influential a critic as Stirling Maxwell is an interesting one which raises key questions as to the nature of the Scots Baronial Revival. It is very tempting to see the revival of Scottish architectural forms as little more than a skilfully crafted deceit, in spirit if not in full intent, which at its worst can be portrayed as no more than an unconvincing imitation. But is Scots Baronial really - quite literally - a damned lie simply because its products imbibe too much or, conversely, too little of the qualities of the architecture of the original castles and fortified houses of Scotland? The inherent contradiction embodied in the question underlines the difficulties of coming to grips with a revival style deriving inspiration from buildings markedly different in rationale from the buildings to which the revived style was applied. Unlike the contemporary revival of English architectural forms during the 19th and early 20th centuries, the Scots Baronial Revival hoped to make use of elements of an historic "style" which was originally not merely domestic, but designed especially with

Formakin - stable court.

Formakin - the old mill.

Formakin - stable court.

considerations of defence in mind. (Even in the early or mid 17th century, height and gunloops usually remained a key characteristic of the lightly fortified houses of the Scottish lairds).

This disjunction between style and function often gave exercises in the Scots Baronial style both an element of the ridiculous in the apparent pretence of a fortified mien (which critics such as Osbert Lancaster have memorably drawn attention to) as well as a certain heightened romantic appeal. Very occasionally, productions in the style wedded the manifestly ridiculous to the hopelessly romantic with such extravagant bravura that they achieved a notoriety verging on celebration.

Formakin - unfinished great hall at sale of Holms' Collection.

First attempts

The eighteenth century saw the first few hints of revival of consciously **Scottish** baronialism as well as very rare statements of Scots Baronial **survival**. Frank Walker has recently drawn attention to the Gordon Tower at Fyvie Castle in Aberdeenshire, probably the most extreme example of apparent survival of pre-classical architecture into the 18th century.[3] The significance of Inveraray Castle (from 1745), Argyll, in the 18th century revival of Baronial (though not specifically Scots Baronial) forms has long been appreciated, as has its essentially Palladian design (however *Gothick* its details).[4] Its central hall, with its soaring internal space and weaponry hung upon its walls, may be a novel enough play on Palladio's Villa Rotonda, but also suggests an appreciation of the grandeur of feudal display. Ironically, while the Duke of Argyll's agents were organising the construction of Inveraray castle, the MacLachlans of Castle Lachlan on the other side of Loch Fyne were rattling their Jacobite claymores in surroundings of genuine and almost barbaric splendour at Old Castle Lachlan which, ultimately, was bombarded into picturesque ruin by a government warship in 1746.

Inveraray Castle.

Despite the general emergence of a castellated Baronial style in the late 18th century and the occasional appearance of Scottish features, it was not until the early 19th century that the first Scots revival houses appeared in the wake of Sir Walter Scott and of the arrival in Scotland of romantic English revival styles. The first attempts at Scots Revival tended merely to adapt the new English styles, grafting on Scottish details such as crowsteps and (rather spindly) turrets.

William Burn, an Edinburgh architect, was a leading figure in the emergence of "Scots Jacobean", as architectural historians now tend to label this idiom. Milton Lockhart in Lanarkshire, of 1829, has been identified as one of the first completely new houses in this vein by Burn.[5] It was immediately copied at Belleisle in Ayrshire, possibly also by Burn. Burn's Ardanaiseig (originally New Inverawe) in Argyll, dates from 1833; essentially the same fusion, although some elements of the design make surprisingly little attempt to adopt a Scottish character. An unexecuted Burn design of several years earlier for Ardkinglas in Argyll was perhaps more successful. It was equipped throughout with simple Scots sash windows rather than mullioned and transomed windows. There were many more such Scots Jacobean houses of this period, and their link with English revival styles, of which they tended to remain but a sub-classification or at best an offshoot, was plain.

Belleisle.

Yet the romantic appeal of Scots Jacobean was considerable, though it was certainly late in emerging in comparison with English revival styles. Novelty, a degree of self-conscious Scottish national identity, and a distinctively "lairdly" association were certainly attractive ingredients. But at root, the new romantic styles, whether Scots or English in the origin of motifs, accorded well with the important task of clothing the carefully devised plan which Scottish architects - and William Burn in particular - were celebrated for at that time.[6] Clients clearly appreciated care expended on creating a house designed to function efficiently for the maximum comfort and privacy of its owners.

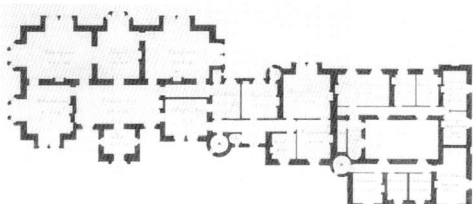

Ardkinglas - unexecuted scheme (RCAHMS).

Ardkinglas - unexecuted scheme (RCAHMS).

Milton Lockhart (RCAHMS).

Carradale.

Carradale House, in Argyll, displays how convenient planning lay as the indispensable essential of such design. Designed by William Burn's colleague, David Bryce, in 1844, Carradale is perhaps best described as Scots Jacobean, and not fully Scots Baronial, simply because of its lack of dramatic massing, its fairly low-key use of baronial features, and its clearly functional composition; all of which characteristics were almost certainly the result of an eye to economy in producing the design. Its harl and much of its detailing, however, harkens back to an earlier Scottish tradition as well as forward to later Bryce houses such as Keiss in Sutherland. Despite the charm of the Scottish features used at Carradale, including
Bryce's clever corbelling-out of canted bay windows to form regular gables above, the basic form of a particularly convenient two storey house is plainly revealed.

In other mansions produced by Bryce (or Burn) in the 1840's, the dividing line between Scots Jacobean and Scots Baronial became more blurred as the detailing (and the loading-on of picturesque features) became more bold and vigorous. Carnell in Ayrshire, designed by Burn in 1843, steered clear of both exaggerated massing and brutalism, but Corraith (now demolished), also in Ayrshire, and designed by Bryce around 1847, had both these characteristics. Tollcross House in Glasgow, designed by Bryce in 1848, is typical of this transition in that, although the compositional massing remains "loose", certain elements mass dramatically to suggest Baronial drama. The square turrets which appear at Tollcross, Carnell and Carradale were presumably derived from Burn and Bryce's experience of Stenhouse Castle in Stirlingshire, which Burn extended in 1836. Turret proportions, however, were generally elongated to suit early Victorian tastes.

Tollcross.

Corraith.

Stenhouse (RCAHMS).

Poltalloch (RCAHMS).

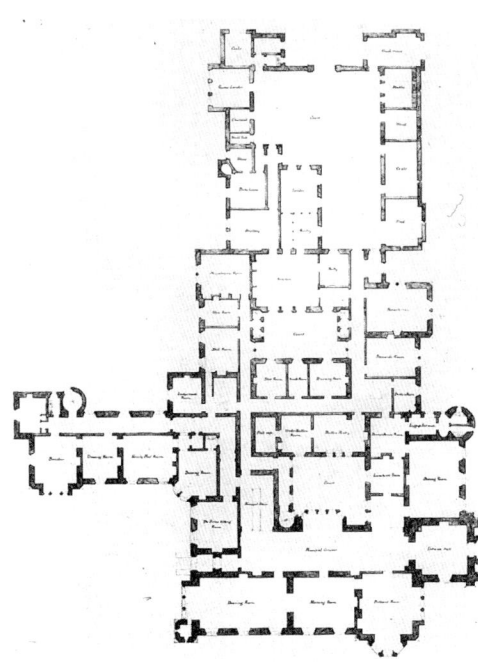

Buchanan - plan (RIBA).

The emerging baronial manner

William Burn, for one, could produce convincingly Baronial detailing and massing by the 1830s,[7] but such exercises seem to have been restricted to additions to old castles, where the tone was already set by the old work and where the intended new work was not required on a scale which would, by necessity, dwarf the old.

Stenhouse Castle in Stirlingshire, mentioned above as extended in 1836 by Burn, is a particularly interesting example (unfortunately no longer extant). Despite the enlargement of the existing castle in an ingenious way by linking a new version of the old towerhouse, Burn clearly had no intention to deceive his audience into believing that new was old. The new work was clearly intended to complement the old, without compromising its own qualities, (suggesting by this date an equilibrium in the architect's mind between the appreciation of old and new).

But Burn's full-blown Baronial manner, seen in Buchanan Castle in Stirlingshire, designed in 1851-53, showed that adherence to the convenient plan types for which he had become celebrated had led him merely to load an almost pre-determined structure with turrets, an imposing main tower, and other stylistic features.[8]

In its bare bones, Buchanan followed the same form as Burn's full scale English Jacobean style jobs; one can see at Burn's Poltalloch, Argyll, (the design of which reached its final form in 1849), the extent to which Buchanan resembled such houses in arrangement of plan and elevations. One can also see, only too clearly, that the English Jacobean style in which Burn normally worked provided a more logical garb for his plan types than did the Scots Baronial he evolved for Buchanan, where the stylistic features were elaborated beyond their usefulness to the plan. His unbuilt and more successful Franco-Scots designs for Fonthill in Wiltshire were more attractive simply because the heavy Gallic seasoning seemed more compatible with the general form of the building. English Jacobean *plus* Scots Baronial might well add up to a passable *Francois Premier*, if handled appropriately!

Inside Buchanan, there was little concession to Scottish sentiment, the most baronial interiors being generally Jacobean of presumably English derivation. "Regarding the use of style internally", Robert Kerr later advised, "a simple and crude Elizabethan would have to be the rule".[9]

It may well have been Buchanan which Robert Kerr had in mind when, in the 1860's, he noted the extra outlay involved in building "the perfectly useless turrets with which the building must more or less bristle", and the main tower usually required when designing in "Scotch Baronial".[10] Spectacular in effect though Buchanan was, and sufficient to satisfy many tastes of the time - in a general sense it probably influenced the design of "the goodly castle of Balmoral" about which Kerr was so (understandably) circumspect - it also exposed the flaw in grafting elaborately irrelevant features to a plan type not readily given to dramatic massing. Playing up to the prejudice of his

Buchanan - garden front (RCAHMS).

Buchanan - entrance front (RCAHMS).

*Scots Baronial architect and laird - James Gillespie Graham
(Scottish National Portrait Gallery).*

*Brodick Castle - drawing room
(RCAHMS).*

Brodick Castle - landing (RCAHMS).

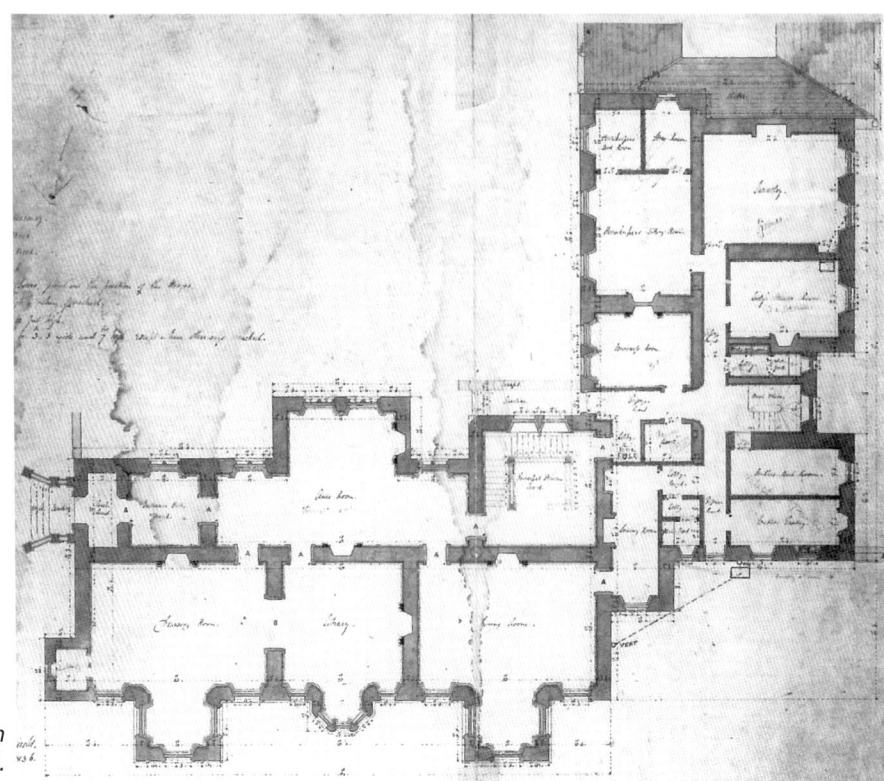

*Stonefield - plan
(RCAHMS).*

largely English audience, Kerr noted that 'we cannot countenance the idea to any degree that the adoption of this admirable plan-model of modern Edinburgh architects is to involve us in an acceptance of the parapets and corbie-steps of the dreary middle ages of the Northern Kingdom...for the mere sake of imitating the obsolete forms of a barbarous style!".[11]

In fairness to Burn, his failure at Buchanan was partly a problem of scale, for his more compact Scots Baronial designs did not suffer from such major deficiencies.

The main tower, so dramatically given expression at Buchanan, is worth watching as a component of revival "castles". An equally impressive and rather more charming version is found at James Gillespie Graham's additions to Brodick Castle of 1844 which (with Ayton Castle in Berwickshire) possibly drew inspiration from Gillespie Graham's early proposals of 1813 for the restoration of the old castle of Blairquhan where such a tower would have been retained.[12] Inside Brodick, the drawing room was designed with a richly ornamented ceiling and a rococo chimney piece - not so dissimilar from Stonefield, as described below - but perhaps due to tight budgetary constraints, the three public rooms were linked by a "passage" rather than the grander corridor halls usually found in work of this period and scale.

An even more individual approach was in fact offered by David Hamilton at Dunlop House of 1831-34. Although it is clustered around a tall entrance tower, Hamilton's Dunlop was dressed in the prodigy style of the late 17th century, as an asymmetrical Drumlanrig; appropriate, surely, in view of the provision of turrets as ornaments, to choose a style which had made them such. Thus the wings - large, bulbous and heavy dormered - hunker round the thin tower, "laced round with strapwork",[13] almost in continuation of a lost style. But the style remained a personal one to Hamilton.

It was neither Burn, Gillespie Graham, nor David Hamilton but the fastidious William Henry Playfair who produced perhaps the most carefully considered and most interesting Scottish Revival house of the 1830's or 1840's, at Stonefield Castle (originally Barmore House) in Argyll. Designed in 1836, Stonefield is a triumph of carefully considered design, providing a unique and genuinely Scottish solution to the characteristic problem of squaring convenience with romance. Horizontal planning and bay windows were combined with baronial drama, through the deceptively simple expedient of combining a baronial, battlemented, tower with a lower wing in the style of a 17th century palace range. That the whole design is informed by scholarship, as well as by great skill in grouping the various elements, accounts for its success.

Playfair's Stonefield evidently derives from a study of Drum Castle in Aberdeenshire, as well as from his own experience gained working on projects around Edinburgh, notably Craigcrook (extended 1835), Bonaly (1836), and Prestongrange (remodelled 1830-31). This gave an apparently easy facility in 17th century (or what was probably taken to be 17th century) detailing, providing a valid means of producing a logical and romantic building, or, at least, one as logical as a romantic building ought to be. Thus the tower at Stonefield, containing the principal staircase, has really only one inconveniently located room. The bay windows, of course, are not canted, but are square projections carried up to gablets above and are

Brodick Castle.

Dunlop.

Stonefield (Stonefield Castle Hotel).

Drum (N.T.S.).

Newark (A.T. Scott).

David Cousin - "Scotch Baronial", 1839.

Maybole Castle.

clearly elegant evocations of the projecting gabled wings of Drum Castle. The gutters are carried across the dormer windows in old Scots fashion, and astragalled windows (associated with old Scottish castles) abound. Glazing bars are even carried around the edges of the windows of the principal rooms to break up the deleterious impact of plate glass.

Inside, stylish compartmented ceilings, suitably Jacobean in tone, adorn the principal rooms. The drawing room, in tune with a taste shared by Burn, Bryce and Hamilton, combines a Jacobean style ceiling with a Rococo chimney-piece.

But despite Playfair's precocious scholarship, convenience is unimpaired, the tower is stylishly "mock", the mansion derived from tradition but its windows opening to allow owners and guests to step on to the terrace. Most tellingly of all, inside one finds an example of the sophisticated planning similar to that which Burn made so much his own, though Stonefield is more than simply English Jacobean in Highland dress: even the leaded ogee roofs which originally crowned the centre bay of the garden front and the flagstaff tower might be considered to have been derived from (amongst other possible sources) Heriot's Hospital in Edinburgh. Stonefield, to re-address our original theme, is neither "poor" nor an "imitation". In fact, Stonefield's exploitation of site and of the potential of 17th century "Old Scots" is in some ways comparable to R. Norman Shaw's "Old English" Cragside in Northumbria of some 30 years later.

Sadly, Playfair's success at Stonefield led only to one further West Coast Scots Baronial commission: a service wing for Islay House, for another Campbell laird. There, the rather agitated jumble of gables and dormers in exposed stone contrasts uneasily with the less frenzied lines of the pre-existing white-harled mansion to which it was joined.

David Cousin, a former pupil of Playfair, did however work successfully in the West, gaining two or three commissions around 1850 to extend and "restore" original tower-houses. Newark in Ayrshire was a major addition to form a country house, "a rumbustious and rampantly baronial affair, bursting with turrets, balconies and dormers ... a particularly splendid house, sober and yet spectacular, lofty and yet competently massed".[14]

Maybole Castle and Kilhenzie Castle[15] in Ayrshire were less obtrusively repaired and extended around 1850, the former certainly, and the latter most probably by Cousin, the relatively sensitive nature of their restoration due to their being intended as a factor's residence and a genteel farmhouse respectively. Had any grander purpose been called for, they would doubtless have received a more drastic aggrandisement.

By the 1850s, Cousin had evidently progressed in scholarship and sophistication beyond the standard of the "Scotch Baronial" design which he had supplied for publication to J C Loudon in 1839.[16] Despite Cousin's astonishing candour regarding his own lack of antiquarian knowledge of the style at that time, one can nevertheless trace a strong affinity with Playfair's work. More significantly and perhaps even slightly alarmingly, in accordance with the lesson taught at Stonefield, Cousin went so far as to spell out in bare-faced prose the deliberate conceit of fabricated (fanciful) chronological agglomeration: "The date of the one part, I think, we may, with propriety, assign to the end of the 13th or the beginning of the 14th century; that of the others (the additions, if we may so call them) to the early part or middle of the 16th century".

Yet, it would be foolish to imagine that Cousin, any more than Playfair, intended to practice serious deception, even when his contrived play with history was expressed with such seriousness.

The same, with a vengeance, may be said of the Scots Baronial work of the Bryce "School" which so dominated the exploitation of the style from the 1850s (or earlier) until the 1870s. David Bryce achieved such success and subsequently such notoriety with the manner he evolved and exploited, that Scots Baronial as a term is often taken as being almost synonymous with his name.

Stonefield - Lodge.

Stonefield - entrance front.

Stonefield - detail.

Kilkenzie Castle.

Craigends - Bryce's Proposals (RCAHMS).

David Bryce

By sometimes planning his houses in a less formal manner than Burn, Bryce[17] was able to tighten up the composition to permit dramatic massing. Formerly unattainable drama became possible and, on plan, seemed even (almost) reasonable. Certainly, thanks to Bryce's skill in the manipulation of massing, it became desirable. This is perhaps Bryce's greatest gift to his countrymen, and real concern with three-dimensional massing often informed the work of his successors. He apparently worked "like a painter at a canvas, returning to the design again and again, adding, changing and rubbing out until the composition was perfected".[18]

In stylistic terms, major elements of design from the old castles of Scotland, culled by way of Robert Billings' *"Baronial and ecclesiastical antiquities of Scotland"*,[19] were ruthlessly adapted to the particular requirements in hand, and an array of detail from two centuries or more pressed into service.

The result of such apparently indiscriminate theft - a tower from Castle Fraser here, an entrance elevation from Maybole Castle there - was not , as one might expect, either chaotic, or simply derivative. In fact, Bryce evolved a coherently integrated and well-defined baronial vocabulary which, despite (or possibly because of) its bold, if brutal, elevational detailing, had considerable stylistic integrity and often startling visual impact. As Kerr observed of Scots Baronial in the 1860s, "to subdue is here to weaken".[20]

Craigends - entrance front before demolition.

This can be seen at Torosay on Mull or in surviving drawings and photographs of now demolished Craigends in Renfrewshire, both dating from the 1850s and fairly representative of an enormous output. The originality of such piles (one largish and the other very large) rests to a considerable extent in the ruthless adaptation to which reference has already been made. Baronial turrets at Torosay wrap round one end of the drawing-room, employed as an ingenious panoramic double bay window (a characteristic Bryce trick, and one to which he resorted elsewhere). Without a sympathy for such swash-buckling vigour, enjoyment of Bryce's Scottish Baronial manner is virtually impossible.

But whatever one's sympathies, Bryce triumphantly overcame the problems of integrating the panoply of the Scots Baronial style with the plan of conveniently functioning houses so that the various features which had seemed to be irrelevant to the plan in Burn's Buchanan, now became largely part and parcel of Torosay, Craigends, and so on.

In plan, both Torosay and Craigends derive, not unsurprisingly, from Burn, with significant modification, but an exposed service basement raises-up the large windowed main-floor to give a more castle-like stance. A main tower again appears in both cases as an important feature, but well integrated into the design as a whole. Although Glenapp (1870) in Ayrshire may have suffered from some paring down of an original scheme,[21] Bryce nonetheless supplied a sturdy towerhouse as the compositional climax, its sheer, soaring stance contrasting with the picturesque huddle of out-buildings at its foot. Its compact plan, raised above an exposed service basement, was typical of Bryce. Yet, on close examination,

Torosay - bay window.

Craigends - as built (RCAHMS).

Glenapp.

Ballikinrain.

Glenapp - staircase (RCAHMS).

Glenapp was simply a variation on the design of Torosay.

No paring down whatever was evident at Bryce's Ballikinrain House (1868), north of Glasgow in Stirlingshire. There, it is said that Bryce "had at last really gone over the top".[22] Yet, however extravagant the enthusiasm, however enormous the scale, Bryce attained as much, if not more, visual coherence than in many a smaller design. Its climax was this time a round tower *a la* Castle Fraser, but sprouting not only the ogee capped Frazer stair turret, but also a high, corbelled, two-storey oriel based on Huntly.

From a utilitarian point of view, the upper rooms of these towers had restricted functional logic (save the housing of unruly batchelors); but they offered a clever compromise with the romantic conceit of a house in the style of a castle. Otherwise, despite a vocabulary of detailing and an assortment of features pillaged from the past (the entrance wing at Craigends is based on the centrepiece of Fyvie Castle), such houses offered well-disposed suites of rooms - public, private and service - which worked well enough to appeal to clients on the basis of efficiency and convenience as well as visual impact.

The high drama of Craigends and Ballikinrain was not, however, matched at Eaglesham (1859) where Bryce provided a large and convenient two-storey mansion with lavishly detailed and well-disposed features, but with little attempt to create bold compositional massing. On a house of this scale, the provision of a three-storey, turreted tower was unhappily inadequate as a compositional device. One assumes that, though the client was prepared to dig deeply into his pocket for enrichment, he did not want to pay for grand gestures. In this respect, Eaglesham represents a curiously opulent regression to Scots Jacobean, with a strong suggestion of Burn's largest English Jacobean mansions and echoes of Pinkie and Bryce's own Panmure at the tower.

Occasionally, Bryce could be swayed to make reference to a local source. Thus, at Broadstone (1869) in Renfrewshire, he introduced both details (especially of dormers and *appliqué* window pediments) and a major design element (the main tower) of nearby Newark Castle at Port Glasgow. But such borrowings were simply introduced and sublimated into the Bryce style like any other source used by Bryce. Broadstone also included a splendid conservatory of distinctly baroque design!

Sorn Castle in Ayrshire, remodelled and enlarged by Bryce in 1864, ultimately took its tone from the surviving old towerhouse, despite earlier plans to introduce conically roofed turrets. Prior to its later remodelling and softening by H.E.Clifford, its front elevation - hard and uncompromising - rose sheer and abrupt from the forecourt, the various wings bound fast into one image by the powerful and strongly corbelled parapet carried around the whole building.

Additions to Dargavel (1849) in Renfrewshire similarly sought to absorb and dramatise the old fortified house which became a large adjunct to the new accommodation. Harmonising the new with the old under a coat of harl, Bryce effectively pulled the towered Z-plan into a new role as part of an integrated and surprisingly subtle play of three-dimensional massing. Though the end effect was again bold, the measures taken to achieve it were by no means clumsy or less than masterly.

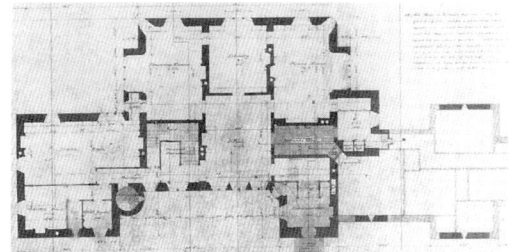
Glenapp - principal floor plan (RCAHMS).

Eaglesham.

Sorn.

Dargavel (RCAHMS).

Torosay - library.

Interiors designed by Bryce rarely took on an affectedly Scottish flavour. Often, as at Torosay, the plasterwork of the public rooms was classical, a baronial flavour perhaps suggested in the interior only by the elements of the owner's decorative scheme which, at Torosay, amounted merely to a second, applied "cornice" of antlers in the entrance hall. A determinedly baronial effect, when such was attempted, was reserved for more public and less feminine areas such as the entrance hall, the main corridor-hall, the staircase, and so on. The drawing room usually incorporated a Louis XVth style chimney-piece. When a baronial flavour did percolate through to the corridor-hall, it was often virtually indistinguishable from the interior work of an English Jacobean style mansion by Burn or Bryce, at once displaying with what ease the Scots Baronial style was employed, and how little it was concerned with archaeological reconstruction.

Torosay - entrance hall (Christopher James/Jarrold).

Craigends - drawing room (RCAHMS).

Craigends - dining room (RCAHMS).

Dalzell - garden front (RCAHMS).

Dalzell - carved detail (RCAHMS).

Dalzell - oculus window.

Billings Baronial

Best known as the author of the four volume *"Baronial and ecclesiastical antiquities of Scotland"*, Robert W. Billings was an English artist and architect encouraged by William Burn to research and illustrate Scotland's historic buildings. Although Burn later withdrew financial support, Burn's colleague and rival, David Bryce, was chiefly to exploit the potential of the illustrations as a source of features and detailing for revivalist houses.

The first use of Billings' drawings as a source may even have pre-dated the publication of the successive volumes. Hospitalfield, near Arbroath, was remodelled and extended by artist-owner and amateur architect, Patrick Allen-Fraser, clearly using Billings as a source with confused if cheerful results. There was little over-all compositional control. Inside, antiquarian tendencies led to some baronial interiors with grand if uncomfortable effect. The contrast with Bryce's coherent massing and essentially contemporary public rooms could not have been greater.

Such literal use of his research did not usually form the basis of Billings' own architecture. When called upon to work in Scots Baronial style, his response was unexpected and quite unforeseeable. His most prominent production was a warehouse development in Ingram and Brunswick Streets in Glasgow; his most successful the design of Castle Wemyss (c.1850) at Wemyss Bay and the enlargement of Dalzell House (c.1857) near Motherwell. Both of the latter, like the former, were designed in Billings' own customary baronial idiom which, though truly bizarre, was also inventive, wild and dramatic.

Castle Wemyss is demolished. The dramatic perspective views - as striking as any in Billings' opus - display a Scots Baronial manner in which quotes from the past are stylistic rather than attributable to specific buildings. But Billings was no "pure" stylist, preferring to derive his own weird idiom characterised by bold and angular (and often ugly) detailing. Stringcourses, in particular, seem to take on a life of their own. More than this, the whole form of the building stepped up through a series of wings, like a lop-sided ziggurat; a progress echoed by the stepped stringcourse, corbelling and offset oriel buttress below.

Dalzell presented Billings with an even more prestigious opportunity than had Castle Wemyss and the nearby Baronial villas of Wemyss Bay, for this was a commission to extend an historic tower and 17th century palace wing. Billings actually lived on site for almost three years, "superintending and working with his own hands" on the "extensive alterations". Essentially, he broke through the south wall of the palace wing to provide a huge bay window running up its face and looking out over an architectonic terraced garden. Meanwhile, the old tower was structurally supported and underbuilt, and large new service additions were appended as well as much interior work carried out. Hardly any of this work attempted to use features from the past as identified by Billings' own research.[23] Instead Billings introduced his own sometimes frenzied conception inspired by the past. Thus, muscular corbelling, zanily shaped window heads, zig-zagging stringcourses, 3-D glazed oculi, idiosyncratic carved detail and, in the stable court, monopitch crow-stepped gables all combined to create an effect deeply personal to its architect.

Within the main floor of the palace wing, Billings created his most spectacular interior, running together two large rooms to create a suite of drawing rooms, richly panelled and with plaster ceilings "wholly the work of Mr Billings, and done by his own hands. Most, indeed, of the new work and stone and plaster was executed by him personally". Small wonder that Billings the author was more prolific and influential than Billings the architect-craftsman!

Castle Wemyss - perspective (Rev. A.A.R. Torrie).

Kilberry Castle.

Largie Castle (RCAHMS).

Antiquarian zeal

Against the mainstream flood of Bryce, his followers, and his would-be rivals, one can detect lesser currents. One of the most interesting of these is a strand of antiquarian zeal which occurred largely in Argyll. Kilberry Castle was rebuilt for the Campbells of Kilberry in 1844 to "celebrate" their enforced retrenchment to their ancestral lands. It was designed by Thomas Brown, whom John Campbell of Kilberry almost certainly came across when Brown was working on the L-plan Lochgilphead courthouse. The laird almost certainly influenced the design of his new house, which differed slightly but significantly from the set of drawings prepared by Brown. His motives were "ancestral", for he "resolved to set himself down on...a bare, flat, featureless, half reclaimed moor...because it was the family place!"[24]

Although Kilberry Castle was in fact cruciform on plan, the approach drive wheeled in obliquely so as to suggest very strongly a tall, L-plan towerhouse. While the turrets were charming dummies (just conceiveably modelled on those at Carnasserie), the projection adjacent to the stair tower (designed to accommodate the W.C.) was astonishingly "vernacular" in quality. Since this did not appear in Brown's initial scheme, it may have been suggested by Campbell of Kilberry himself. The wheel staircase, later altered, was intended as the principal stair of the house from the start. The interior was quite plain, with classical chimney-pieces.

Kilberry was not alone. The 1857 rebuilding of Penkill in Ayrshire for its antiquarian inclined laird of ancient name - Spencer Boyd of Penkill - was apparently designed by the enthusiastic laird in cahoots with a structural engineer: in this case a lethal combination! The result was certainly zealous, but unconvincing, apart from the portions of the formerly ruined castle which were incorporated. Nevertheless, as at Kilberry the house was planned around a spiral stair. It's interiors, unlike Kilberry's, were, or subsequently became, decidedly Baronial.

Of such houses, Largie Castle in Argyll (1857-59) was the most thorough, offering a completely new castle rather more impressive than the diminutive ruin of the real one nearby. Whether the MacDonald Moretons actually wished visitors to believe their home to be a genuine 16th or 17th century castle seems unclear. Certainly, they went to a great deal of trouble to contrive an effect which, externally at least, could just about be taken for the real thing. What is certain, however, is that the owners traced their pedigree from Somerled; an ancient and impressive descent which might have seemed to demand a seriously Scottish castle. Regrettably, Largie was pulled down in 1953.

Largie Castle's plan displays the inconvenience the MacDonald Moretons were prepared to face in the cause of a spurious but nonetheless admirable quest for antiquarian authenticity: the house was one room thick throughout, had no real corridor-hall, and centred around a large wheel-staircase where, according to tradition, the laird would constipate the routine of the house by lecturing his gamekeeper there each morning. It would never really have done in a house by Burn where "every minutiae of the habits of the gentry" was catered for!

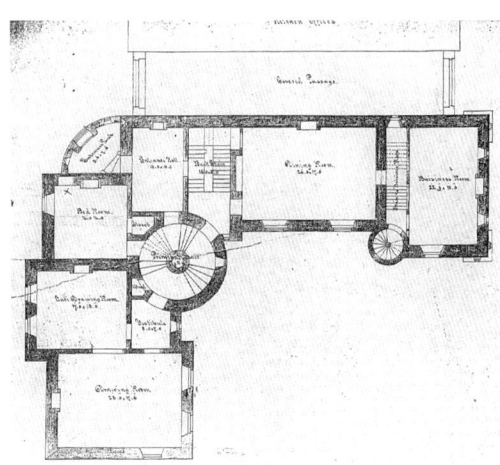

Largie Castle - plan (RCAHMS).

Kilberry Castle c1854 (John Campbell).

Largie Castle (RCAHMS).

Inverawe.

Dunmore.

Largie appears to have come from the office of Charles Wilson, a first-rate Glasgow architect who usually worked in classical styles. However, it seems also to have been this office which extended Inverawe House (1850-51) for the Campbells of Inverawe, principally by formally baronialising the vernacular towerhouse with the addition of square turrets with gabled roofs (as on the lower wing at Largie). Inverawe's baronial tower has since been cut down in size, a significant commentary in itself on the utility and convenience of this high-rise baronial pile.

In 1857, Charles Wilson & David Thomson "restored" Duntreath in Stirlingshire. Later antiquarians found the antique complex "somewhat altered", though little enough is known of their work here since it was later overtaken by further remodelling.

Elsewhere, Wilson's office was less than fastidiously antiquarian in approach and , although Robert Billings' *Baronial Antiquities of Scotland* was clearly pillaged - Rutherglen Town Hall is largely based on the view of part of Fyvie - the end effect was scarcely antiquarian in any serious sense. At Shandon House in Dunbartonshire, Wilson's picturesque panoply of turrets and towers was scarcely serious. Lastly, as far as Wilson is concerned, the tall towerhouse of 1862-64 at Benmore in Cowal, Argyll, appears to be from his office though it lacks the conviction of Largie or Inverawe. It is curious that its style, with spindly, tall-roofed turrets, should have been so crankily bogus when such trouble had been taken to raise such a lofty gesture to antiquarian feeling.

Dunmore is yet another mansion in Argyll designed to suit strongly antiquarian tastes. The main house, now a burnt-out shell, took the form of a rectangular towerhouse with, on the whole, relatively small windows puncturing the sheer walls. In fact, it was a remodelling, probably carried out around 1850, of an earlier Georgian "box".[25] The building of a service range parallel with the former front of the mansion not only created a courtyard, later filled in, but attempted to disguise the previous character and orientation of the house. With the exception of the awkward junction of the crowstep gables oversailing the parapet-walk, the result was reasonably successful.

Skipness House,[26] Argyll, designed in 1884 by John Honeyman, did incorporate a towerhouse but only as part of a considerably larger and highly convenient mansion. Even so, it did form the dominant feature in views of the house, much of the sprawl being hidden by its L-plan layout. The same was the case at Honeyman's earlier Achamore House (1876) on Gigha where a harled version of the same tower had appeared. Skipness' interior included some work in a Jacobean or pseudo-Scottish Baronial taste not too far removed from Osbert Lancaster's wonderful send-up of Scottish Baronial interior design. Be this as it may, the taste for mock towerhouses was, even among the old gentry families of Argyll, largely focused around the mid-century period; by the 1880's the taste had largely passed, though its ultimate spiritual successor - castle restoration - was to be even more obsessively concerned (as we shall see) with adjusting the needs of the present to the character of the past.

Outside Argyll, there were really very few examples of 19th century antiquarian zeal as far as the building of principal estate residences was concerned. In the West, Dunbartonshire has two border-line cases: Drumhead and Cove Castle. Both adopt an upright stance. Drumhead, of around the 1840s by an unknown architect, certainly rises tall, but convenience is scarcely impaired. The latter is more striking, with its elegantly proportioned drawing room suite on the top floor, as if to permit both good views and the placing of an oriel window in an appropriately high position. However, Cove Castle, with its detailing reminiscent of J.T. Rochead, is clearly explicable as a marine villa - almost a holiday home - rather than as an ancestral symbol of an ancient family.

Cove Castle.

Skipness.

Benmore.

Arden.

Auchendennan.

Kilmahew.

Achnacloich.

The Bryce style triumphant

The enthusiasm which created these remarkable antiquarian inclined houses did not even dent the triumphant reign of the Bryce Baronial style. Even architects such as John Thomas Rochead, a former Burn clerk (and designer of that most virile Scots Baronial rocketship, the Wallace Monument, near Stirling), and Andrew Heiton of Perth, himself a former Bryce pupil, designed in idioms which, one feels, capitalised on the success of the Bryce formula, while varying and personalizing it more than a little. Rochead employed a muscular baronial at Blairvaddich (1848-51) and an entertaining if not deadly serious embattled baronial at Levenford and its lodge (1853) in Dunbartonshire, while Heiton at Giffen House (1869) in Ayrshire designed in his customary, spiky (and somewhat horrid) idiom of that period.

J. Burnet (senior) was perhaps a little further from the High Victorian Scottish Baronial norm, creating at Arden (1868) in Dunbartonshire an eclectic and barely Scottish confection. Kildalton (1866-70) on Islay can also be ascribed to Burnet (senior), though evidently "directed" by a committee of taste of the owner and his friends; "directed" to save money, to judge by the lack of picturesque detail.[27] The thin irrelevance of the main tower is certainly reminiscent of that at Arden. The mix was scarcely improved in additions to Newfield (pre 1880s) in Ayrshire, though Burnet (senior's) best baronial chateau - Auchendennan (1864-66) in Dunbartonshire - is (with his Kilmahew House (1865), also in Dunbartonshire) closest to the Scottish Baronial consensus of the time, despite a Romanesque-style porte-cochere and some Franco-Scots exuberance on the entrance front.

While Burnet (senior) could produce work of the very considerable qualities of Auchendennan, others were less talented. James Smith's Overtoun (1859) in Dunbartonshire, for example, is lavish but less well handled.

Of the Bryce "school" itself, as one may term those architects most closely linked with him in their training or much influenced by him, Peddie & Kinnear[28] were the most active in the West (in fact, in Argyll): a garden front of the 1870s for Kilberry is a pared-down Torosay (a block of efficiently disposed rooms, but given real massing by the careful grouping of a few features); the notorious Glengorm (1860), clinging jagged and crustacean-like to a bleak headland on Mull, has a "garden" front overlooking the ocean which expresses its obvious layout of main rooms with indelicate panache; and Gruline (1861), a fairly monumental shooting lodge (also on Mull), masses compactly around a corner tower. Back on the Argyll mainland, Achnacloich (1885) is very likely the best domestic work of John Starforth, another former Bryce pupil. It is a lively composition reminiscent of the manner of the master.

Curiously, Wardrop & Reid,[29] who were significant in the further development of the Bryce idiom in the East of Scotland, appear not to have designed any Scottish Baronial mansions in the West, though they did manage a congruous addition to Robert Adam's late 18th century "castle" at Culzean. The now

Glengorm (RCAHMS).

Glengorm - entrance front.

Kilberry Castle.

Gruline (His Grace the late Duke of Atholl).

Ederline (RCAHMS).

demolished Ederline House (pre-1871) in Argyll may possibly have been their work, though Peddie & Kinnear themselves or Rennison & Scott would represent a strong possibility of authorship. Ederline was in fact a masterly piece of work, with the device of a tower on the entrance front enlarged into a great towerhouse surmounting the lower huddle of public rooms and service wings. Such imposing drama did not, however, compromise either the functional serviceability of the building (only the upper floor of the tower might be deemed excessively inconvenient) or the integrity of the Bryce style. However suggestive of authentic massing the silhouette may have been, the handling - particularly of surface treatment and detail - remained robust, vigorous and shockingly brutal, as can be seen in the indelicate mastery by means of which planes are gratuitously advanced and recessed around the corners of the lower wings, as if the building were made of so much cheese!

If Ederline made a virtue of boldness, Dunselma, overlooking the Holy Loch from Strone near Dunoon, pushed the Bryce style to its extreme limits, raising aloft an exaggerated tower engorged with extravagant Brycean vigour. Since Dunselma, designed by the Paisley firm of Rennison & Scott in 1885, was apparently intended as "a sailing lodge" for one of the Coats family and commanded a wide panorama of the Firth of Clyde, there is perhaps some excuse for a tower which had begun to resemble a lighthouse. But to push the Bryce style beyond this limit could only lead to absurdity.

In 1920, an unsigned article in "*The Scots Pictorial*" (describing Peddie & Kinnear's Gruline) fairly sympathetically hit at the nub of the Brycean stylistic approach: "the house follows in its style the old Scottish type of architecture, say of the middle of the 17th century, with rounded tower and crow-stepped gables and other features; but it does not profess to be of that period".[30]

Rather in opposition to Lorimer's later witticism at Formakin, Gruline proudly (and characteristically of its type) bore the inscription "D.G., 1861". "D.G.", of course, represented the initials of the owner, not a faintly sardonic quip. It also bore the monogram of its architects.

Dunselma.

Drawing room by Peddie & Kinnear.

Seafield.

Franco-Scots Baronial

Despite the evidently widespread belief of the time that Scottish architecture of the 16th and 17th centuries owed its unique form to the action of French influence upon native tradition, Bryce and his fellow travellers were not overly eager to employ their own amalgam except, curiously, in public buildings: Greenock Sheriff Court of 1864-67 by Peddie and Kinnear is a West Coast example typical of the taste. Such exuberance and elaboration was as nothing, of course, compared with the *ne plus ultra* of Franco-Scots taste: Fettes College in Edinburgh of 1864-70, designed by Bryce himself.

Seafield in Ayrshire is perhaps not untypical of the excess which the injection of French frolic *orne* could bring to a more sober tradition (though, in truth, it is deportment rather than detailing which suggests France). The present appearance of this showy pile was largely due to alterations of 1858 by Thomas Gildard. But (if one excludes the entrance front of Auchendennan) virtually the only significant example of Franco-Scots Baronial applied to a country house in the West is Dunans in Argyll.

Dunans.

This mansion, dating from around 1864[31] (though an older, smaller house is at least partly subsumed), is thoroughly impressive and quite breathtaking in impact. It is a house designed to be seen along a single, controlled approach: as one crosses a ravine on the drive it suddenly appears, a distant but stunning vision which dominates the view as one curves up to its terraced setting and across its forecourt. Its architect is unknown and its detailing suitably bold, relying on extremely effective massing culminating in a tall tower with an open "round" clinging, lamprey-like, to its upper works. Although it is clearly High Victorian in tone, it is not quite from the Bryce stable and has a certain single-mindedness about its visual impact which marks it out as a particularly powerful design. There is nothing of the fanciful "toy castle" about this composition, despite a lavish equipage of pantomime gunloops.[32]

Dunans.

A Second Revival?

Surprisingly little was written at the time about High Victorian Scots Baronial - it spread by example rather than by theory - and what little was written could be critical. The style was hardly taken up south of the border, so much was it identified with its own cultural context of dirks and sporrans. Unlike the Victorian Goths with their championing of moral, religious or national themes, the architects of the Scots Baronial Revival had no such earnest program, and remarkably few qualms over designing in a variety of other styles, so that even to name them by this single style might give a misleading impression. If anything, they took as their guiding light the fitting of romance to "the common comforts of residence" and, towards this end (as we have seen), reduced "the ultimate standard combinations" of design elements to a system. This was initially achieved by "certain Scotch architects", and it was principally William Burn whom Robert Kerr had in mind in making this observation.[33] But it was David Bryce and the generation who trained with Burn and with Bryce which heightened the romantic appeal through the means of achieving both a convincing asymmetry of dramatic massing - on occasion as stunning as a sledgehammer blow between the eyes - and a "modern", bold treatment of detail and composition which could not be mistaken for work of the 14th, 15th, 16th or 17th centuries.

All this changed as the end of the 19th century approached and the Arts & Crafts movement made itself felt in Scotland: there was a discernible move away from Brycean romantic brutalism towards a more suave handling of detail and of form. Also discernible in some cases, by the early 20th century, was a precise interest in exploiting the textures and handling of old Scots castles for nostalgic purposes, or else, more rarely, in streamlining their forms as part of a more *avant garde* approach. And in a more all-embracing sense, the influence of the Arts & Crafts movement was profound, though Scottish architects on the whole tended to respond to its manifestations rather than to its philosophy, hence the number of exercises in English Manorial and Yeomanorial styles which began to spread throughout Scotland in a welter of delectable half-timbering and hanging tiles from the 1880s onwards.

Perhaps the most effective way of visualising the change in treatment of Scots Baronial or "Old Scots" subjects by the early 20th century is simply to compare the turrets of Bryce's Torosay with those of Lorimer's Dunderave. Though part of a restoration of a real late-16th century towerhouse, the turret roofs of Dunderave are entirely Lorimer's own conception and, with their adoption of the spirit of the old, emphasise the essential divergence from Bryce's treatment. This is, however, a more extreme contrast than was often the case.

In fact, a few exercises in High Victorian Scots Baronial taste continued into the late 19th and early 20th century - The Ross near Hamilton, designed by Alex Cullen (of all people) in 1894 is a good example - but their retrograde design served only to underline the manner in which tastes had changed. Even The Ross, it has to be said, was equipped with a sleek baronial entrance hall with more direct reference to the past than Bryce might have placed in an interior.

So widespread was the change, it is possible to see the later

Dunderave (RCAHMS).

The Ross.

The Ross - entrance hall.

Glencoe House.

Islay House.

Arrochar Hotel.

history of the Scots Baronial revival as a progression towards a greater understanding and sympathetic adoption of the genuine qualities of the original style, and in this Robert Lorimer is generally considered the leading figure: "Scotland will not achieve what England has already achieved - a completely national style of house-building based on the old vernacular architecture - until it follows the lead given by Lorimer", wrote Hermann Muthesius in 1904.[34] And with this understanding comes the idea of a Second Revival and the creation of "a true neo-vernacular architecture that rejected Baronial pomposity and concentrated on the simple dignity of solid masonry construction and the reduction of Baronial cliches to simple, sensible , culturally resonant forms".[35]

Scottish architects - some a good deal more than others - were indeed "stirred by the wind of modernity",[36] and strove to interpret a national style based on the "charm of unpretentious old Scottish buildings, with their honest plainness and simple, almost rugged massiveness".[37] The concept of a Second Revival is undeniably useful in describing this general change. However, the snappier term, "stripped baronial",[38] is not always appropriate since turrets and such features remained much in evidence.

Robert Rowand Anderson is usually seen as a path-finder for the Second Revival. His Glencoe House of 1895 was certainly an example of "stripped baronial", with its emphasis on "bare solid walls and proud gables - the essential characteristics of real old baronial".[39] Alas, it was also rather dull, although it composed well when the garden front was seen from a distance. In general massing it may be seen as a precursor of Formakin. Its original red-tiled roof "was so glaringly foreign"[40] that it has been replaced with Ballachulish slates. In fact, Anderson's important Glasgow public buildings of Pollokshaws Burgh Hall (1895-98) and the Govan Pearce Institute (1902-6) were better by far: careful, scholarly and restrained, their fitness of form for purpose overlaid with judiciously selected Scots Renaissance ornament.

Later, in 1910, Anderson's Glencoe House was simply outclassed in avoidance of Baronial pomposity by Detmar Blow, a leading English Arts & Crafts proponent who extended Islay House (on Islay). Blow succeeded in adding a new wing (almost as large as the existing 18th century main block), carefully and deferentially stepping back his addition and tactfully hiding Playfair's service wings which were, in fact, the only "baronial" elements of the whole harled and crowstepped pile.

Lorimer, as we shall see rather later, was important because of his return to first principles to derive a modern Scottish Arts & Crafts style. But there were other figures who often worked in Scottish styles, some of whom had enjoyed a *beaux arts* training in Paris. And at the lowest level, there were those who simply took on, second-hand, the spirit of the age with, to be honest, a surprising degree of success (viz., Frank Burnet & Boston at Fa'side House (1903) near Newton Mearns).

A.N. Paterson's own home, Longcroft (1901) in Helensburgh was a much publicised exercise by him in harled Arts & Crafts taste. Since it bulged with towers, turrets and other protrusions in a rather Leiperian composition, it can scarcely be called "stripped" in the way that his Arrochar Hotel might, but it did nonetheless capture something of the feeling of an old Scots fortified house, without any suggestion that it was other than of its own period. Longcroft's interiors were noticeably "artistic", though not *avant garde*. On the other hand, internally, historic style was actually no more than faint allusion, with little more than panelling and an arched screen in the hall to maintain the theme.

In the same breath as Longcroft, one can mention J. Jerdan & Son's Balnowlart (1905) in South Ayrshire, John A. Campbell's Southwood (1905) in Troon, T.A. Millar's Silverglades (1912),[41] also Troon, and his Boghall (1907-8) and Bankell (1907-8) near Milngavie.[42] Equally, George Washington Browne's Langlees (1899) in Lanarkshire, if not too far inland for this survey, might be included in this category of houses strongly influenced by Arts & Crafts taste.

Longcroft.

Langlees.

Baronald - interior of hall (RCAHMS).

Southwood.

Duntreath (RCAHMS).

Baronald.

Dougarie - unexecuted tower.

Duntreath (Lady McGrigor).

Muthesius, in his 1904 study of "*The English House*", did spare a few words for Sydney Mitchell, though his exercises in Scots Baronial style did not seem to merit examination. In fact, the work of Sydney Mitchell & Wilson was curiously mixed in character. Their 1890 treatment of Duntreath Castle in Stirlingshire has recently been described as "a mixture of vandalism and flair"[43] with an enormous collection of buildings inserted into the complex and much historic work devastated. Its scale was impressive and dwarfed the old towerhouse. Closer to Bryce than advocates of the Second Revival might wish, Duntreath was intended to operate upon the senses of the beholder in much the same way as Bryce's largest Scots Baronial piles. On the other hand, Sheilbridge House (1898) in north Argyll (now Inverness-shire) was harled and sophisticated in the Arts & Crafts manner. Glenborrodale (1898-1902), like Duntreath, was more grand - almost High Victorian - in effect. While its entrance front was a mass of corbels, battlements and dormers, the bulk of the garden front comprised a huge tenement-like tower with engaged corner towers inset like bay-windows; a daring re-interpretation of Huntly, perhaps... or simply (as with the corresponding feature at Niven & Wigglesworth's Kincardine House (1894-1906) in Kincardineshire) a derivative of James Maclaren's 1887-9 Stirling High School extension!

John James Burnet, foremost amongst those trained in Paris and son of John Burnet, is not usually remembered for his Scots Baronial or Old Scots designs, excepting the most splendid Fairnilee (1904-6) in the Borders. Nevertheless, Scots-style with Burnet tended to involve a rather grand, faintly Baroque handling of Scottish forms, as found at Baronald (1890-91) in Lanarkshire or at Garmoyle (1890) in Dunbartonshire. Baronald, one feels, is two rather good houses trying to burst out of one design, while at Garmoyle the composition is fused to one, but with less success. Edinbarnet (1885-9) is unfortunately cut down in height following a fire in 1975. Burnet's interiors might veer towards a skilful contemporary baroque in their handling of detailing, even when the actual motifs were Jacobean or occasionally even Celtic. Burnet's Scots Baronial style undoubtedly influenced the 1911 remodelling and enlargement of New Castle Lachlan in Argyll. Killean House near Campbeltown was probably completed in the early 1880s(?) by the young J. J. Burnet and is actually a rather more interesting building than Baronald, with a subtle entasis to the entrance and garden towers; though it is possibly too Ruritanian to be considered Scottish in inspiration.[44] The unbuilt towerhouse for Dougarie on Arran, envisaged by Burnet in 1894, was composed of box-like elements, its proto-cubism offset by a corner bay which may also be influenced by Maclaren.

Silverglades.

Balnowlart.

Killean.

New Castle Lachlan.

Killean (Argyll & Bute Library Service).

THE ORIGINS OF THE SECOND REVIVAL

The earliest manifestations of the "Second Revival" lie outwith the West of Scotland.

R.Rowand Anderson early applied restraint to houses such as his own Scots home, Allermuir (1882) in Edinburgh. Previously, the 1869 restoration of Castle Stewart in Inverness-shire by J.M. Wardrop, and Prof. Lorimer's restoration of Kellie in Fife from 1878 had both adapted old castle-mansions with minimal alteration.

The experience of finding Kellie Castle on a family walk would not have been lost on Prof. Lorimer's 13 year old son, Robert; nor would the experience of slow and exacting restoration of the house's many attractive features have been any less formative an experience. Later, while training with Hew Wardrop and with Anderson, Lorimer was sent as site agent in 1885 (following Wardrop's death) to another early example of Arts & Crafts influence, Place of Tilliefour. This extension to a small 17th century house was a rambling two-storey affair which opted for picturesque charm rather than baronial grandeur, creating a new interest in vernacular forms.

Towards the end of the 1880s, James Maclaren attracted attention with his High School of Stirling extension of 1887 (in the form of a sparsely detailed baronial tower) and with his work at Glenlyon Estate in Perthshire in a variety of British vernacular idioms. Glenlyon Farmhouse was the most interesting: an extraordinary Arts & Crafts tour de force, but scarcely Scottish despite the harl. In its freedom of vernacular expression there was a suggestion of the route C.R.Mackintosh was later to explore.

By 1901, Lorimer had moved from Bodley's office in London to that of Maclaren's successors, Dunn & Watson (Maclaren having succumbed to tuberculosis). In 1891 Dunn & Watson produced Fortingall Hotel on Glenlyon Estate, a genuine Arts & Crafts revival taking real joy in the accurate transcription and sensible re-use of the quieter forms and features of pre-classical Scotland, with an implication of gradual agglomeration. It summed-up in a moment the potential of a truly domestic architecture based on the vernacular, much as R.N. Shaw and W.E. Nesfield had done for England since the move in the 1860s away from aristocratic English Jacobethan towards the more seductive charms of the half-timbered manorial and "Yeomanorial" styles.

By 1892, of course, Lorimer was back in Scotland on his own account, beginning his first great restoration at Earlshall in Fife where the client was probably motivated by what Lorimer's father had done at Kellie. Shortly afterwards, Lorimer was working at The Grange in North Berwick, daringly mingling Scots and English vernacular forms. By 1895, therefore, Anderson's Glencoe House was clearly advanced, but not leading the trend.

One of the less well-known architects of the age seems to have been Charles S.S. Johnston who is well worthy of interest, if only as a specialist who, in the West of Scotland, was called in by clients who had a house - sometimes a real baronial house - which they regarded as not quite baronial enough. At Woodside (1890) in Ayrshire and at Pollok Castle (c.1891) in Renfrewshire, Johnston created stylish yet complementary towerhouse cores in Arts & Crafts influenced taste, either to recreate a lost feature, or simply to provide the compositional massing and symbolic power missing from the existing historic building. At Barochan (additions of c1898) in Renfrewshire, Johnston's wing evidently gave so much pleasure that later owners knocked down everything else. At Peddie & Kinnear's Glengorm on Mull, the fact that Johnston carried out remodelling of the inner hall and staircase in 1911 is certainly not visually evident, so well did he fall into an impeccable Brycean style.

So much then for the largely Arts & Crafts inspired Second Revival as it manifested itself in the West of Scotland. From the sample of the work of the more significant architects described above (excluding Lorimer who will be dealt with later), it must be clear that, rather than forming a single movement, the apparent attempt to take on something of the character of old work clearly broke down into a number of broader themes and, ultimately, individual approaches. Harl, softer handling and a sensitivity to the charm of the time-worn may often have been employed, but if the Brycean consensus had been formed in the image of Billings' dramatic perspective views, the Second Revival did not so obviously re-invent the style in the image of MacGibbon & Ross' "Castellated and Domestic Architecture of Scotland", however influential this five volume study may have been in widening understanding and experience of the original baronial style and its "art qualities".

Pollok Castle.

Barochan.

Beyond the Arts & Crafts movement

One architect who did read MacGibbon & Ross was the young C.R. Mackintosh who made use of their work in his lecture on baronial style. In recent years, research, neatly summed-up by Gavin Stamp, has suggested that: "Mackintosh's inventive architecture was deeply rooted in Scotland. Look again at the Hill House: is it not streamlined Baronial, complete with turrets? Look at the dramatic side elevations of the School of Art: are they not castles? And then there is the extraordinary harled back elevation of the Art School.[45]....a modern, stylised Baronial pile as abstracted and as truly Romantic as Castle Drogo. It has everything to do with the Baronial impulse of the Victorian Age and very little to do with the un-romantic 20th century."[46]

This is not, of course, to suggest that Mackintosh was purely inspired by Scottish Castles and vernacular buildings. They are simply one important ingredient and are perhaps most clearly seen in the simplified forms of one of his unbuilt schemes for Auchenbothie Gate Lodge in Renfrewshire: L-plan, shorn of crowsteps and conical roof but with quaint guttering, water-butt and a staircase tower in the re-entrant.[47]

Perhaps in the hands of Mackintosh, baronial and vernacular influence (pressed into service in a new cause at the Hill House, Windyhill or even in the towers of Scotland Street School) had become as new, novel or "modern" as it could without ceasing altogether to carry with it associations of the original style. As it was, Mackintosh's advance beyond Arts & Crafts, his extraordinary and often unhistoricist interiors, his striking originality and his relationship with the most advanced movements in continental and British art (not to mention his "cubist volumetric expression") placed him quite beyond the bulk of public understanding and, indeed, of the aspirations of all but a handful of clients. However influenced he may have been by old Scottish castles, Mackintosh's style was not that of those he termed "these modern antiquarian sentimentalists"[48] for, unlike them, he was not an Old Scots baronialist but a New Scots architect.

It would be heartening to suggest that Mackintosh's treatment of the exterior of his domestic commissions formed part of a wider movement in Scottish architecture. It would hardly be true. In the West of Scotland, the work of Morris & Hunter in Ayrshire produced simply modelled mansions which blended Tudor and Old Scots under a coat of harl, as at Black Clauchrie (1898) or Templetonburn (1901 & 1908), but although interesting and quite advanced, these houses were English first, Scottish later, and not terribly much more.[49] By its subtraction rather than addition of revivalist detail, M.H. Baillie Scott's The White House (1899) in Helensburgh may possibly have been an influence on Mackintosh.[50] Certainly, those few houses, such as James Findlay's Ballumbie (1906) near Dundee which introduced fenestration with similarities to that of Mackintosh, tended to yield in other respects to a picturesque if cranky Arts & Crafts version of a Scottish fortified house.

In fashionable Southwood at Troon, several long grey-harled houses - one of which, Crosbie (1908), is by H.E Clifford - are

Hill House.

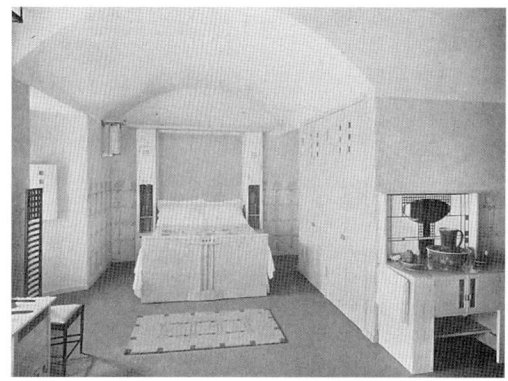

*Bedroom at Hill House -
echoes of towerhouse interiors.*

interesting in that their form simply expresses their plan, plainly and without fuss. The other, earlier house, Lochgreen (1905) by Gardner & Millar, was in fact merely a toned-down version of a scheme by John C. McKellar. Presumably in both cases design was influenced by a desire for economy. If Mackintosh's client at The Hill House was at all influenced by such considerations, what he got for his money was, of course, a different matter. Clearly, Mackintosh did not form part of a Scottish movement in this sense. He had plunged beyond Scots Baronial and stood largely unadmired by his contemporaries in Britain, and quite alone.

Kinlochmoidart (RCAHMS).

Glendaruel.

William Leiper

It would be quite wrong to leave the subject of Mackintosh's "successful" contemporaries in the West of Scotland without considering the work of William Leiper. From as early as the late 1860's, Leiper had been an exponent of a more sensitive approach towards designing in what he probably preferred to call "Old Scots". He also developed a similar facility in "Old English" houses. So easily recognisable - or so frequently used - were Leiper's favourite motifs, features and even general composition or plan that the term "Leiperian" was coined. Amazingly, much of his later work in Old Scots, including the general grouping of elements, is foretold in his first Scots Baronial (or Old Scots) mansion of Colearn (1869) in Perthshire. Thereafter, the composition was developed and fine tuned somewhat exclusively in his West Coast mansions (for he was a Glasgow architect who lived in Helensburgh).

Of these, Dalmore of 1873 in Helensburgh, is his most successful. It was worth repeating, and was repeated, albeit on a larger scale, much further north at Kinlochmoidart, in 1883-84.[52]

Not only were Leiper's sources often more rarefied than those of Bryce, and his architecture undoubtedly influenced by self-consciously aesthetic considerations, but also the logic of the convenient plan is not so immediately obvious externally and, in general terms at least, appears sublimated to the composition as a whole. As Frank Walker and Fiona Sinclair have noted of Dalmore, "the bare scattering of windows" imparts "a grand, impregnable effect".[53]

Auchenbothie in Renfrewshire, now a vandalised but ultimately almost indestructible shell (thanks to its concrete floors), was designed by Leiper in 1898 and represents a further development of the type, now clad in the harl of Arts & Crafts taste, but corresponding closely to the existing formula in layout and massing. On this occasion, a low service wing was pushed out to form a third side to an implied courtyard adjacent to the entrance. Glendaruel House in Argyll came later, but the difficulty of incorporating an existing house restricted Leiper to some extent, so that this mansion is dominated more than usual in his work by a single, principal elevation.

Beneffrey (1910) in Glasgow came later still, but this is the work of Leiper's acolyte and second brain, William Hunter McNab. McNab may possibly have been a better architect than Leiper, but since he coined the term Leiperian and did not depart from this idiom even in work entirely his own, - he named his son William Leiper McNab - he and Leiper must effectively be considered emanations of a single source. That McNab ultimately assisted, co-partnered and succeeded to a man whose art was allegedly "of too personal a nature to submit to the trammels of co-partnery"[54] is indeed a telling point.

In point of fact, McNab's Beneffrey eschewed ostensibly Scottish detail such as crowsteps, though the pivotal compositional device of round tower, balanced by assorted other features, remained strikingly correspondent to the above mentioned Old Scots essays. Beneffrey has been described as "very much the kind of thing a rich American connoisseur of the period would have favoured".[55]

Dalmore (without original glazing).

Auchenbothie (before recent redevelopment).

Auchenbothie - service wing.

Kelly.

Drawing room at 18 Park Circus.

Though Red Tower (1898) in Helensburgh and Kelly House (finished by 1891) were both by Leiper, they share with Beneffrey an ambiguity of style. Red Tower is simply a fusion of Leiperian "Old Scots" and "Old English", but Kelly is more difficult to categorise. Its style might best be described as Franco-Scotto-Anglo-Dutch! Its life was cut short in 1914 when it was burned down by suffragettes...and why not?

Kelly House suggests that Leiper's greatest weakness was that more might mean too much: an excess of funds available for a project brought out the worst in him. In this he was the antithesis of the moral tale told of Robert Rowand Anderson who, when asked what he would do if required to spend more on an already fine room, replied "I should make the walls thicker".[56] What Leiper did do under fairly similar circumstances is illustrated by a drawing room at Park Circus, Glasgow, remodelled in 1891. Although it is in fact very good, there is a distinct feeling of excess.

Ballimore.

In a scheme of alterations and additions of 1898 at Ballimore House in Argyll, Leiper was forced into "entirely transforming its aspect"[57] (from 1830s Tudor Gothic into Leiperian Old Scots) without actually demolishing the house. Leiper was thus compelled to use the existing format of a main entrance elevation looking down an avenue of trees towards Loch Fyne; effective enough, though a distinct move away from the more compact, three-dimensional coherence of his earlier (completely new) Scottish houses. In this respect, houses such as Colearn, Dalmore, Kinlochmoidart and Auchenbothie had achieved one of the most characteristic qualities of the old towerhouses of Scotland's 16th and 17th centuries. Nevertheless, as was observed of Ballimore as long ago as 1919, Leiper's vocabulary of "ancient features" was used frankly and "without a pretence of being ancient."[58]

In compensation for fitting his work to an existing structure, Leiper employed at Ballimore a virtual directory of his customary external ornament, from telescopic corbelling (previously used at Colearn, modelled with the visual quality of firm rubber cushions), through ornate 17th century-style dormer-heads, chimneys set diamond-wise, and a variety of favoured finials, to the almost sculptural mannerist monument placed atop the bay window of the inner hall. This *Francois Premier* feature also appeared, with greater justification, on Leiper's Sun Life Building in Glasgow, as did much else emblematic of a slightly disturbing desire to quote from art works of the Italian and French Renaissance.

Knockderry.

Of all Leiper's work, his 1896 addition to Knockderry Castle in Dunbartonshire is probably the most dramatic: a towerhouse of imposing scale, with a rich, colourful interior. Externally, by balancing full height oriels with flanking, smaller windows (as was also done at Glendaruel), the impression of impregnability was not compromised.

Leiper's interior design was of a high order. More careful and considered than that of Bryce, it often incorporated wood panelling of high craftsmanship (sometimes running to linenfold carving). Frequently fireplaces and sideboards were recessed in timber panelled and framed alcoves, and fireplace lintels and arcaded screens sometimes treated with a wide, ogee arch. Windows, where not chunkily astragalled, were often leaded in elaborate patterns, as found in French chateaux[59] as well as

Leiper interior in 17th century taste.

Ballimore - addition.

Red Tower.

Auchenbothie - garden front (RCAHMS).

closer to home. The general atmosphere was usually dark and rich, enlivened by colours in carpets and occasionally by dazzling, stencilled wallpaper. The effect was no more specifically Scottish than in the houses of Bryce, but it **was** Leiperian and the sometimes occurring synthesis of dark panelling, gothic fireplace, embossed wallpaper, and stags' heads created a tangible atmosphere now more redolent of the Victorian Scottish Baronial home than the work of those who were not so "free from a pedantic archaeology".

It is no surprise that the best, most Scottish, Leiperian interior was by William Hunter McNab: the highly attractive baronial hall at the rear of Chalmers' shop in Oban (destroyed by John Menzies shop). This subtle interior of c.1909, barrel vaulted in light coloured timber with panelled walls, ribs resting on corbels, and an array of fawn stags heads, was simply a delight, one of the best "theme" interiors of its time, and one of the finest products of the Scottish Baronial Revival.

McNab not only produced this Oban interior, but also the highly satisfactory tenement block of Argyll Mansions (1906-09) which incorporated it.[60] With faceted francophile corner tower, clusters of chimneys set diamond-wise, subtle polychromy with contrasting texture of stone, and very Leiperian Scottish pedimented dormers, the whole confection is carried aloft on an arcade of pink granite columns. It is certainly one of the highest quality tenemental designs in Scotland, outclassing even J J Burnet's excellent Scots Baronial tenements in Campbeltown.

It was probably also McNab who added the delightful extension to Ballimore around 1914, creating another sophisticated exercise in a very personal idiom with less than direct reference of motifs to the past: the ogee-roofed stair-tower, reminiscent to some extent of Robert Lorimer's work, might be based on the stair-towers of The House of Gray near Dundee (which also had raised margins) or, indeed, on Leiper's largely "Old English" Ardchoille, Dunbartonshire, of 1901.

It may almost be true to say that Leiper designed only one Scots Baronial mansion, and subsequently modified the design on a number of occasions. In so doing, by the last years of his life the charming old aesthete had managed to run the whole gamut of taste from the 1860s until the Great War without ever seeming less than stylish. It is a shock to realise that Leiper's Scots Baronial work, which seems so thoroughly "Edwardian", has its unmistakable origins at the beginning of his career, almost half a century before.

It may also be true that Leiper, despite his early development and familiarity with English architects including William Burges and J L Pearson, did not contribute much to the development of Scottish architecture: he had no real school of followers, and his practice simply fizzled out in the years after his death. Though he neither looked back to near-authentic reconstructions of the past, nor forward beyond a subtle synthesis of historic styles, Leiper has a select appeal which continues to attract a small but enthusiastic audience. He is now, notably, one of the very few architects habitually named in estate agents' newspaper adverts...a dubious yet interesting distinction.

As an architect member of the Building Committee of Glasgow School of Art since 1894, Leiper would have been familiar with C.R. Mackintosh and his work in some detail.

What he made of it is not known, but he was not influenced by it. To Mackintosh, Leiper was perhaps not merely another "modern antiquarian sentimentalist"; as fellow aesthetes of differing generations, they would have had something in common. Presumeably John Honeyman, with whose firm Mackintosh worked and whose baronial houses of Achamore (1876), Skipness (1881) and The Cliff (1900) were not too dissimilar from the work of Leiper, also held some value in the estimation of the young Mackintosh. According to David Walker, "Skipness showed that, given the right client, Honeyman could come close to beating Leiper at his own game. In its skilful Arts & Crafts style use of rubble-work it was rather ahead of its time, and even anticipated the Wardrops' experiments of a few years later in producing houses with more of the qualities of the 16th and 17th century originals...".[61] At Mugdock Castle (1883) in Stirlingshire, James Sellars (or Campbell Douglas?) masqueraded as a coarsened Leiper with less success than Honeyman. But whatever affinities the work of Leiper may have had with these and other British architects such as John Douglas of Chester, his game was matched across the Atlantic where architects such as Henry P. Kirby of New York had arrived at a seductive Francophile Baronial without a native style of their own upon which to draw!

Argyll Mansions (MacArthur Stewart).

Sketch by Henry P. Kirby, 1891.

Dunderave - library (Lord Weir).

Dunderave - a bedroom (Lord Weir).

Dunderave in its setting (Lord Weir).

Castles restored

And so, with the phenomenon of castle restoration, we return to Robert S. Lorimer. Lorimer's approach embodied the sensitive revivalism of the Arts & Crafts movement, combined with a sentimental or nostalgic appreciation of the spirit and details of old Scottish houses. His restoration of Dunderave of 1911, like his work at Formakin, beautifully embraced the spirit of the old builders, taking on some of the feel and texture of old work.

For contrast (and in revival of 17th century arrangements), the new wings were grouped to suggest a courtyard, but left open so that a view into the L-plan of the tower was offered from the approach. The visitor then entered the intimate courtyard, with its various textures of cobbles, walls and roofs, through the dark enclosure of the entrance pend[62] which may have been inspired by that at Gylen Castle near Oban.

Stone slabs were used for the roofs. The turret roofs were given a subtle bell-cast, contrasting with the almost clumsy heaviness of the great slabs as they seemingly strove to mould themselves to the turret contours, creating an effect both contemporary (and very "Lorimer") yet also suggestive of the hand-wrought character of the old work.

Inside Dunderave, wandering through rooms with exquisite ceilings playing on not merely the style but also the sweet irregularities of the 17th century plasterwork, one can scarcely fail to be moved by the sensitivity and sheer joy of this most careful of revivals.

Dunderave - view into courtyard.

Dunderave.

Plan of Dunderave.

Dunderave.

Dunderave - before restoration.

Kirkland.

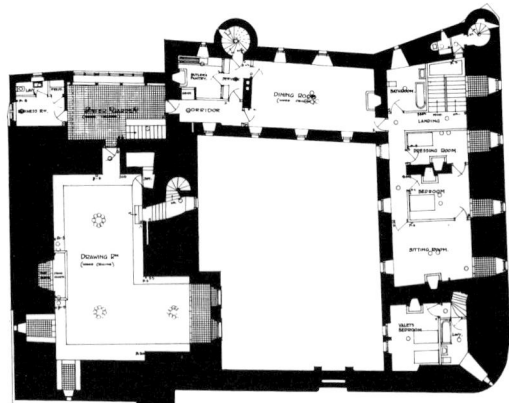

Duart - plan.

Lorimer was not alone in the sensitive restoration of ancient castles, restorations which on the West Coast in the late 19th and early 20th century seemed to forgo standard notions of convenience with even greater gusto than those antiquarian mansions of the mid-nineteenth century! One Mr Butters of Perth was called upon to sensitively restore the exterior of Barcaldine in Argyll between 1896 and 1910, initially without harl, and even equipping the windows with yetts hinged open in the event of fire. The result was small with a rather ham-fistedly recreated Great Hall, but probably comfortable enough. Its owner, Sir Duncan Campbell, had purchased it back as a ruin; it had been temporarily lost to his family since its sale in 1842.

Even smaller was Wester Kames Castle, a turreted tower reconstructed rather than restored by Robert Weir Schultz in 1896-1900 for Lord Bute, but not for his residence. A line of red tiles marked with true S.P.A.B. honesty the junction between old and new, though the new was "based on no concrete evidence of its original appearance other than comparison with similar buildings."

One of the sweetest of the smaller restorations was Kirkland in Ayrshire, a crowstepped house restored (c.1895?) and later extended (1910) for a Dunlop cheese merchant by James Chalmers.

Duart Castle on Mull, restored by J.J. Burnet around 1911-12, was a little less cosy than Barcaldine or Wester Kames, though every effort was made to utilise its extensive courtyard layout to provide proper service facilities suitable to the relatively efficient running of such a pile. Nevertheless, Duart remained a little hard around the edges. However, the original structure (with all

Barcaldine today (with harl).

Wester Kames.

Barcaldine as restored.

Duart under restoration.

Dean under restoration.

Eilean Donan.

Eilean Donan - the tower.

the difficulties of plan that it entailed) was very little added to and only adjusted rather than rebuilt internally. Its situation, atop a cliff on a bare headland, would have been outlandish for a residence by, say, mid-Victorian standards, but its unspeakable romance was doubtless compensation enough in view of the clannish enthusiasm of its 75 year old 27th Chief, Sir Fitzroy MacLean, who had repurchased the castle and a little of its peninsula immediately before work began. The MacLeans had, incredibly, lost control of Duart as long before as the 1690s. Duart falls only narrowly short of being a Scottish Lindisfarne made more potent by clan associations.

Dean Castle, Kilmarnock, where restoration directed laterly by J.S. Richardson continued almost until 1945, ultimately became a museum. For Lord Howard de Walden, the fastidious aesthete for whom both the tower and palace range at Dean were restored, restoration and reconstruction provided a fascinating pastime. The provision of fighting platforms round the courtyard walls underlines that more than merely domestic requirements were being taken into account!

Begun in 1912, George Mackie Watson's virtual rebuilding of Eilean Donan in Kintail for John MacRae-Gilstrap offered inconvenience on a hitherto unwished for scale. It was finished as late as 1932. Allegedly, restoration began "with the help of Farquhar MacRae", a crofter "who had seen in a vision the ruined stronghold restored to its former glory...Every detail of the restored structure was faithful to the original which was revealed to Farquhar MacRae in his dream...".[63] Though the serious historian may balk at such highland mist (and in particular at claims of "authenticity"), Eilean Donan is certainly not to be assessed within the narrow parameters of archaeological terms. It represents, in the very real substance of stone and mortar, an equally legendary vision, motivated once again by clan considerations and, first and foremost, belief in one's own propaganda: the MacRae Gilstraps of Conchra believed in their ancient clan heritage to the extent that they were prepared to recreate it.

Eilean Donan's "Billeting Room" and "Banqueting Hall" were both dedicated to the worship of unplastered rubble. Despite the near barbaric splendour of the latter, there is something almost camp in the affectedly crude stonework of the canopy to the fireplace! The same might be said for the "olde world" bridge which links the castle with the mainland.

Yet Robert Lorimer had outdone all these monuments or hobby-restorations through a rigorous attention to texture and finish, conjuring up a perfect idyll of the past. At Dunderave new beams were "roughly finished with the adze to lose any irregularity the saw might have left".[64] Here was not merely the dramatic creation of atmosphere conducive to a dream of the past, but the creation of that very quality of age which made old buildings so desirable. Here was "instant age", the critics cry. Here, if anywhere, is the "damned lie"?

Lorimer's work has certainly been "damned"! He has been seen as occupying the end of "a defunct tradition", and Thomas Howarth succinctly declared that "his positive contribution to architectural development is questionable". More recently, Charles McKean declared that "Lorimer went back into the past and, for the most part, stayed there"[65], an assessment all the more damning because it is at least partly true.

Duart - a bedroom.

Duart (RCAHMS).

Sir Robert Lorimer.

But should we assess work merely in terms of its contribution or irrelevance to the evolution of modernity? Even during World War One, while he worked on Balmanno, it can scarcely have seemed to Lorimer that he occupied a dead-end in architectural history. To Muthesius, who published in 1904-11, it seemed that Lorimer offered "a completely national style of house-building based on the old vernacular architecture", [66] and a modern style at that.

Certainly, it is fair to say, as Hussey has said (with rather cloying adulation), that Lorimer admired "the refreshing qualities of things made by men's hands, lovingly with an old song in their hearts".[67] whether this damns Lorimer, negates his achievement, or gives him a perpetual niche in architectural history, is rather a matter for personal philosophy. Perhaps, once again, we shall come to value more widely the qualities of national architectural tradition, of natural materials and of hand-hewn craftsmanship, and perhaps even be openly sentimental about them. Standing in the courtyard of Dunderave in Argyll, one would have to be a priggish philosopher not to feel sympathy, and a tinge of sentiment, for Lorimer's vision.

Ardkinglas from the approach.

Barely in the present?

Even if Lorimer's work need not be "damned" by posterity, does it remain, by definition, "a lie"? Unlike Burn, Bryce, Leiper or Mackintosh, did Lorimer take on the spirit of the past to the extent that his creative achievement barely remained in the present?

Stirling-Maxwell, mischievously quoted at the beginning of this essay, also stressed that although Lorimer could take on the spirit of the old work to the extent that observers were momentarily "staggered", his buildings "were in no sense copies. No one who **examines** them could possibly mistake them for old buildings"[68] [my emphasis].

One sees this most clearly at Ardkinglas, a new mansion designed by Lorimer in 1906, where "he even omitted such characteristic features as the gable chimneys".[69] This was not all, for Ardkinglas was clearly not laid out to replicate the form of an old castle or 17th century mansion. Its great delight, apart from its interiors, is in the complex three-dimensional harmonies of its elevations. Its roofs, likewise, flow into one another in a way which echoes - or so it is said - the undulations of the mountains around.[70]

The view on the approach to Ardkinglas before the drive turns towards the house, is one of the great moments of Scottish architecture. At this point, as the house comes in view, the disparate elements of the design merge to form a unity, building up in layers or tiers from the service wing, through the two storey entrance wing, to the three storey main house - itself a composition of many groupings - and the tower above. Ardkinglas perfects what Lorimer first attempted at Rowallan (1902) in Ayrshire, There, the brutality of the High Victorian designers was drowned in a welter of "eye sweet curves", Art Nouveau styled dormers, and graceful, even mellifluous, lines of gables and turret roofs. While Ardkinglas maintains much of this visual elision, it comports itself much more compactly than Rowallan and, being less literally composed as a revived fortified house than Formakin, is the most original and successful of Lorimer's three great "Scotch" mansions.

This is most evident on the south facing elevation of Ardkinglas, rising strongly above broad terraces overlooking Loch Fyne. There is none of the corresponding longitudinal sprawl of Rowallan, dying away into lower service wings, nor the abrupt rising of Formakin like a tower house, straight from its parkland. Rowallan carried unmistakable echoes of 17th century Auchans Castle, most effective in the oblique view where much of the house is hidden, while Formakin expressed a more thoroughly fortified grouping. Even the lower service wings at Formakin formed an enclosed approach which had to be pierced by an arched gateway to reach the forecourt. On the entrance front of Formakin, the composition may even have become a little too complex. Ardkinglas, in contrast, merges a series of vertical elements in an almost abstract composition of forms (pierced at one point by an arcaded loggia), yet tied down to revivalism by disciplined, though flowing, use of historical detailing. Consequently, seen distantly from across the Loch,

Ardkinglas.

Ardkinglas - steps to terrace.

Rowallan.

Ardkinglas - the saloon.

Formakin - plan.

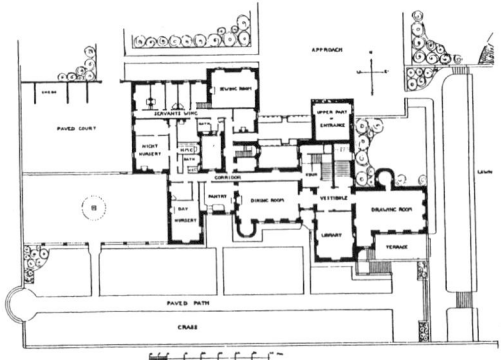

Rowallan - plan.

Ardkinglas seems like a different design, its style and emphases indistinct once the various inflections are lost in the general haze.

What matter that inside Rowallan and Ardkinglas one finds beautifully sensitive evocations of 17th century plasterwork? Lorimer's upbringing with its central event of the repair of Kellie in Fife by his father (Kellie was discovered in sumptuous and almost French dereliction on a family walk when he was thirteen) imbued Lorimer with a lifelong love of the qualities and texture of 17th century craftsmanship and design. But such loving variations on an antique theme merely adorned interiors which - unlike those at Dunderave - were manifestly "modern rooms" which fitted into a modern plan within a modern revivalist design. Deceit was not an issue. Delight was all.

Even with Formakin (where the plan was pared down and strung-out so that a more "authentic" Old Scots massing was possible, even when viewed from a distance at which detail was blurred), the intention was to recapture qualities and associations rather than to posture in deceit. The whole point of "D.L." was that it was intended as a joke, in much the same way that Lorimer inscribed above the door at Rowallan, "*Deus Pascit Corvos*": *God feeds the crows*, or in Old Scots, the **corbies**: his clients for Rowallan being the **Corbett** family.[71] Similarly, John Holms, the client for Formakin, appreciated or even demanded the play on the date. Incidentally, the estate was called "Formakin" (a name which has puzzled scholars into obscure Gaelic etymology) simply because Holms assembled it from farms *for makin'* a garden and a house. (It is surprising that Holms did not have "Holms Sweet Holms" inscribed above his fireplace: instead, he chose the text, "God bless the rich for the poor can beg".[72] But this was in his "temporary" accommodation nearby, for a financial loss prevented Holms from installing Lorimer's scheme for the interior at Formakin).

Lorimer's adherence to the Arts & Crafts movement on grounds of conviction and inclination together with his interest in revivalist architecture - often for wealthy dilettantes - made him anything other than a pioneer of Modernism. Though he did not attempt to replicate the past, it and its associations strongly influenced his work because of their inherent value to him. If Lorimer's craft was architectural nostalgia, he elevated it to an art form.

Formakin - fireplace detail.

Formakin - Lorimer sketch.

Dunderave - ceiling dated 1911 (RCAHMS).

"Moderne" Scots Baronial?

After the Great War, the Arts & Crafts movement began to visibly fail. One symptom was the paucity of new mansions in Scottish styles, though a number continued to be built in English styles. Its cause was the general inclination, stronger than even before the war, towards Arts and Crafts **effect** rather than Arts and Crafts **process**. Nonetheless, the restorations of Eilean Donan and of Dean continued to inevitable completion like the stamp collections of millionaires! On the other hand, the democratization of Arts & Crafts influence in the extensive council housing schemes of the inter-war years - almost always variations or even repetitions on English Domestic themes - only further diluted rather than intensified the Arts & Crafts approach.

Against this, the emerging new *moderne* styles offered an idiom free of associations with feudal power, landed wealth or even rural tradition. "A design stripped of associations of the past may have the effervescent charm of novelty, but is a dull lifeless thing,"[73] warned Sir John Stirling-Maxwell. In his "*Shrines and Homes of Scotland*" of 1937, Stirling-Maxwell went so far as to present an illustration of untypically convincing Old Scots public amenity housing above the caption "MODERN COTTAGES". But, in theory at least, there could be common ground. If "architectural simplicity and functionalism was characteristic of Scots architecture",[74] the removal of period details might leave "a simple stone structure with exciting projections".[75]

In practice, such a compromise was scarcely practical for with period details removed (and *moderne* features installed) it would be difficult to distinguish an Old Scots derived design, unless baronial height and massing were used. Keil Hotel, built on the Mull of Kintyre in the late Thirties,[76] though not a country house, did suggest such a rapprochement between tradition and modernity: built with a keep-like tower with a bay-windowed "palace wing" adjacent, the whole is reminiscent of Kilbirnie Castle in Ayrshire, perhaps, or even Drum in Aberdeenshire. Seen obliquely from the curving coastal road, the composition has considerable power, its rounded bays rippling across its facade. Such instances of baronial reference were, however, very rare.

MODERN SHOOTING LODGE

MODERN HOUSE   MODERN COTTAGES

"Shrines and Homes of Scotland".

Keil Hotel - designed by J. Austen Laird.

Drum towers on thirties housing in Renfrew.

Modern castle restoration

After World War Two, whilst the Scottish market for new country houses of any size or prestige seized-up almost completely, the restoration of old Scottish towerhouses and fortified houses - most of relatively modest size - gradually took on a new lease of life. By the late Seventies this had become an established trend, a measure of grant aid from the Historic Buildings Council having been available since 1958.

Throughout Scotland, over seventy castles have now been restored since the last war, and there is little sign of the enthusiasm abating while potential restoration projects remain. However, the rise and rise of castle restoration has remained a minority interest, isolated from the mainstream building habits of the day. Despite this, castle restoration has undoubtedly involved a far larger number and wider social variety of individual restorers than of yore. Few such clients have been traditional owners; the majority were not, nor have become, landowners or farmers on any significant scale.

Enthusiasm and the relatively modest means of some restorers have led many clients to indulge in "hands-on" restoration to a greater or lesser extent. Some have even been their own "architects".

The most influential of all modern restorers have been the sculptor, Gerald Laing, who restored Kinkell in Ross-shire from 1969, and Mike Rowan, who restored Mains in Lanarkshire from 1976. Laing's book, "*Kinkell, the reconstruction of a Scottish Castle,*" and Rowan's T.V. documentary established castle restoration as a seemingly attainable ideal (even among those who could not afford it).

Whatever the motivation of these modern restorers, and however obvious the link between castle restoration and architectural conservation, it would be wrong to assume that all castle restorers and their architects fit neatly within the philosophy of modern conservation practice or even within the best restoration approaches of their own decades! Almost all restorations, beyond simple consolidations, involve major intervention, and restoration can consequently seldom be seen as "archaeological" reconstruction, much less as repair. It must instead be viewed as another chapter in the history of the building, for better or worse. As with Lorimer's Dunderave, the process will hopefully make the building more rather than less significant to the architectural historians of the future. "Already the heady times of reconstruction recede", wrote Laing in 1984, "and become merely one incident in Kinkell's long history".[77]

In opposition to the situation prior to 1914, modern restorations have predominantly grouped in the East rather than the West of Scotland. Despite this, the West can offer both continuity with the past tradition of clannish and hobby-restorations, as well as providing some instances of high quality work.

Deprived of the lavish budgets of Edwardian millionaires, it is curious that some of the castle restorers in the West of Scotland

Castle Stalker (RCAHMS).

have continued to restore large and difficult structures in spectacular but inconvenient settings. Kisimul Castle, an early 15th century (if not earlier) tower and enclosure, rising almost directly from the sea on an island in Castle Bay, Barra, was bought back by R.L. MacNeil of Barra in 1937 and restored between 1958 and 1970. Scarcely intended for permanent modern occupation, and certainly not suited to it, Kisimul was simply patched-up and some domestic buildings within the courtyard were rebuilt for occasional residence.

Though not of such unyielding a nature as Kisimul, Castle Stalker was likewise located upon a small island off the Appin mainland and, though of apparently mid-16th century date, was of a strongly defensive and vertical character. It was restored in the later 1960s by Stewart Allward, a Surrey solicitor. Allward had more in common with the new breed of castle restorers than had McNeil with his ancestral motives. After an initial flirtation with the services of Ian Lindsay, Allward proceeded with neither architect nor contractor, hiring labour and carrying out considerable work himself while motivating others into voluntary efforts. In order to work on their castle at weekends the Allwards were in the habit of driving 13 hours **each way** from Surrey.

The exterior of Stalker, viewed from the mainland, seems impressively authentic. Rebuilding was relatively minimal and far less conjecture or compromise was necessary in reconstructing the form of the roofs than at Kisimul. The interior was brought back to life in a more personal way. Breacacha on Coll, likewise supposedly of the early 15th century, was similarly restored without the constraints of Historic Buildings Council assistance.

Though not underway to any significant extent, Alex Fleming's proposed restoration of Carrick Castle, (a very early and large tower in Cowal), to the designs of Ian Begg and associates, is sufficiently ambitious in scale and remote in its (mainland) location to group with the restorations considered above. So daunting is the size of the tower that the owner intends to occupy for domestic use only an imaginatively reconstructed later addition and, ultimately, further living quarters in the attic of the tower. As is now the case at Dean and Eilean Donan, the main rooms of the tower, if completed, will presumably be for public inspection rather than residential use.

Outwith this category, the remainder of restorations in the West of Scotland correspond closely with the general run of restorations elsewhere in Scotland. Most have been of relatively modest size, convenient location, and comparatively late design. Mains at East Kilbride, restored by Mike Rowan, is a slight exception in that it is a 15th century tower with the bottom two levels poorly lit so that the useable accommodation inconveniently begins above this level. Rowan's resourceful 1976-79 restoration minimised obvious intrusion and reconstruction as far as possible, not even replastering his stone vaulted Great Hall and concentrating most innovations within the rebuilt attic storey. Although he used both joiners and stonemasons, he did a considerable amount of skilled work himself, including manufacturing leaded glass windows, making a bathroom suite from beaten copper(!), and (with friends) hauling up beams, which he had thoroughly adzed, into place. Architectural services were provided by John Wetten Brown, who subsequently worked with other strong-willed "hands-on" restorers.

Kisimul.

Kisimul - rising from the sea.

Carrick Castle.

Aiket.

Blackhall - interior view.

Saddell Castle.

Carried on simultaneously with the work at Mains was Robert Clow's reconstruction of Aiket in Ayrshire. This was very different from Mains, involving complete reconstruction (due to extensive structural problems) above the level of the vaulted ground floor, permitting a conjectural return to the supposed early 17th century form of the building. Although there were many clues to suggest what this form would have been, Aiket is in fact not only the most winsomely attractive of restorations, but also one of the most impressive exercises in revivalism in Scotland. Clow designed the reconstruction himself as his second project as an amateur architect. He had previously reconditioned a house in France of similar date, which may explain the almost French air of Aiket; French in the same sense that Traquair is almost French. Indeed, the dormers in the low wing at Aiket were modelled on those of Traquair.

The interior of Aiket, with a marvellous combination of exposed stone details, smoothly undulating plasterwork and exposed timber beams, is an exemplar of the quality which castle restoration can achieve; such a style also finds fluid expression in David Pearson's excellent 1984-89 restoration of Castle Leven at Gourock with Raymond Muszynski from Ian Begg's office as architect. Leven, a reasonably convenient double tower of late 14th to early 16th century date, did not require to be so extensively rebuilt as Aiket, though a new conical roofed turret provided a stylish climax to its massing.

The later Begg commissions in the West were sadly not to be so productive: at Law castle in Ayrshire, restored from c.1987, the restorer dispensed with their services at an early stage (and has yet to complete the restoration); and at Dunduff, also in that county, the restorer asked for (and got) new upper storeys to a ruin which may in fact never before have been completed. Compared with Aiket's renaissance, that of Dunduff - without crowsteps, turrets and with a curious short ration of chimney stacks - might leave a suggestion more of what might have been done rather than what was actually done.

Though not a restoration in any sense, Ian Begg's Raven's Craig in Wester Ross, built for himself from the late 1980s, is strongly influenced by Muckrack in Inverness-shire (which Begg restored c 1975). Raven's Craig is not merely a reproduction towerhouse, though at times it comes close. Planned for modern life lyrically adjusted to vertical living (with provision made for future installation of a lift), it agrees with the firm's prospectus for "the erection of very good buildings able to carry tradition forward"; an Arts & Crafts ideal, perhaps, though not quite Arts & Crafts in its expression at Raven's Craig. Some motifs are deliberately without precedent and the materials are often unashamedly modern. Particularly successful are the turnpike staircases where the newel posts around which the stairs revolve are omitted and replaced by a void which almost attains the physical presence of the absent newel: "as I was going down the stair I met a newel that wasn't there..."

Not all restorers in the West have been private individuals, however. The Landmark Trust's restoration of Saddell castle in Kintyre, using David Carr as architect, exemplifies the long and evolutionary building history of this castle. Since only a little more than honest repair was called for - the towerhouse was derelict rather than ruined - the Trust did not break with the evolutionary character, opting instead for a restoration of Victorian restoration of a remodelling of the 16th century! The latest period of work produced some good, congruous interiors.

Mains.

Leven.

Saddell Castle - interior view.

Blackhall - D.I.Y. restoration.

Newmilns Tower (S.B.P.T.)

Kilmartin Castle - prior to restoration.

The recent restoration of 16th century Lady Cathcart's House in Ayr to the designs of Simpson & Brown for The Scottish Historic Building Trust is scarcely a castle but instead a much-altered example of a town residence. Nevertheless, it is worth consideration here if only because of the similarities of the challenge, from vaulted cellars to conjecturally "reconstructed" crowsteps and dormer-heads.

Certainly the most individualistic restoration has been that of Blackhall in Paisley, restored during the 1980's by Alex Strachan without Historic Buildings Council funding, and using John Wetten Brown to provide architectural support. Following Mike Rowan's example, this lecturer turned D.I.Y. restorer managed almost exclusively to utilise his own and other voluntary labour, reconstructing the missing stonework, rebuilding crowstepped gables and re-introducing missing dormer pediments. In his rehabilitation of the interior, Strachan introduced his own freebooting personality, re-using fragments of architectural stonework and other features saved from Paisley buildings prior to demolition. These were incorporated in the interior without undermining the general effect, but also without camouflaging too deceitfully their alien origins. Thus, a huge rough-dressed archway appeared in the entrance area, Victorian panelling from demolished Brediland House appeared in the dining room, and a portion of neo-gothic parapet railing acted as a lavabo in the Great Hall. Such atmospheric eclecticism was backed up by an upper chamber in Old Scots taste, itself largely formed from salvaged items, and by plaster vaults in the ground floor recreating the general ambience of the long-gone stone vaults.

Two ancillary buildings for Blackhall - a stone double-garage, and a delightful garden house largely constructed from re-used plinths for balustrading - complete the ensemble. Since the ingenuity of the garden house's construction remains visible, it seems all the more appealing.

At present time, Kilmartin Castle in Mid Argyll is under restoration by an enthusiast - using Crerar & Partners as architects - who has already rebuilt a fallen gable. Just finished, is the restoration of Newmilns Tower in Ayrshire by Ian Cumming for Strathclyde Building Preservation Trust, with stylish Glasgow architects, Page & Park, handling the architectural control of the project. Cumming is a professional enthusiast whose capacity for building and repairing in stone at competitive rates is much valued (although, in this case, the solution to the problem of badly eroded stonework has been lime harl).

Like his nearest equivalent, Major Mike Tait, Cumming has in the past worked exclusively in the East of Scotland. Involvement at Newmilns has brought him a further task in the consolidation of ruined Dunure Castle in Ayrshire. A similar scheme of consolidation of a ruin is underway at Gylen Castle on Kererra, off Oban, for which S.P.A.B. man Martin Hadlington from Bob Heath's office is architect. Ian Begg, of course, has similarly consolidated the ruin of Castle Moil on Skye.

With the careful repair of ruins as archaeological exhibits one veers, of course, from revivalism or indeed "architecture" towards simple preservation. Perhaps the most elaborate preservation exercise in the West of Scotland has been the dismantling and rebuilding of the ruin of Loch Doon Castle in South Ayrshire to save it from being submerged in an enlarged reservoir. This happened as long ago as the Thirties.

Blackhall.

Blackhall - the dining room.

Gylen - under consolidation.

Despite the variation in approach and quality of modern restorations with re-occupation as residences in mind, almost all have in common an end effect which tends to deny its own time: the most telling sign of the best of restoration work tends to be its self-effacing zeal. In respect of exterior appearance, this approach is almost universal. Interiors impose greater problems for restorers, not least because of the compromising introduction of modern conveniences (has anyone ever reverted to 15th century plumbing?) but also because, with all original plaster or woodwork usually absent at time of restoration, the interior may present the restorer and his architect with a largely blank canvas. The general desire is clearly to use this opportunity to design with a "period" flavour, though exactly which period can be difficult to tie down!

Recently, a young architect working in Glasgow declared his intention to complete a set of historic rooms: "So far", he declared, "I've been allowed to do a few 14th century interiors at a castle near Aberdour".[78] "Doing" the 14th century, or more accurately, "doing" the 14th to 17th centuries has long been a delight open to castle restorers which increasingly few are able to resist. Within the modestly sized Great Halls of Aiket and Leven, this atmospheric character attains an extreme of excellence. It is only because of the utter improbability of so "complete" and so congruous a set of interiors having survived that one recognises that all must be new. Lorimer's "damned lie" has been perfected amid coats of smooth but undulating plaster applied like butter, and beams genuinely worn with time because they have, in a previous existence, supported a pier or a mill floor. What matter that one may change century as one crosses from one room to the next, thanks to the preservation of "original" features of different dates. What matter that in one fortified house one opens a characteristically rough boarded door to reveal a more sophisticated neo-17th century interior with the door's inner face panelled! What matter, indeed, that furniture of more than one century and chunkily astragalled windows may combine to add to the total effect. When interiors of such atmospheric appeal are created, the fact of their existence is its own justification. Such interiors, like the restored husks which contain them, do not really represent a scientific reconstruction of the past, detached from the march of time. Instead, they represent a creative revivalist conceit, and therein lies their considerable significance. However much Historic Scotland has fussed over items of detail - to perhaps insist on reversion to leaded rather than astragalled windows, to agonise over harl mixes, and to debate whether or not to harl up to or over the rolled or chamfered mouldings - castle restoration, like the revivalist idioms of the past, has not generally been motivated by the quest for "authenticity" but simply by the desire to carry conviction in its own terms.

Rebuilt arch within modern restoration.

Interior of a restored great hall.

Interior of a restored great hall.

A moral dilemma

Oscar Wilde once observed that there is no such thing as "moral" or "immoral" books; a book is either well written or badly written. The same might apply to castle restoration but for the fact that, since the time of William Morris, the treatment of ancient buildings has been seen by some as having a "moral" dimension. According to Morris' 1877 manifesto for The Society for the Protection of Ancient Buildings, ancient buildings deserved to be protected and handed down "instructive and venerable to those who come after us". Morris asserted that "of all the restorations yet undertaken the worst have meant the reckless stripping a building of some of its interesting material features; while the best have their exact analogy in the restoration of an old picture, where the partly-perished work of the ancient craftsmaster has been made neat and smooth by the tricky hand of some unoriginal and thoughtless hack of today". Instead of restoration, Morris pleaded for the treatment of ancient buildings "as monuments of a bygone art ... that modern art cannot meddle with without destroying".

Although in his restoration of Earlshall in Fife, Lorimer - himself a member of S.P.A.B.[79] - managed to escape criticism for substantial intervention through re-touching the gallery ceiling,[80] modern restorers have recently come under fire in the aftermath of the 1992 Architectural Heritage Society of Scotland Conference, "Restoring Scotland's Castles". Organised by Robert Clow, the conference intended to provide a retrospective review presented by a selection of castle restorers or their architects. Immediately, the difference between professional conservation philosophy and the philosophy of many restorers became evident. In the aftermath, the variety of standpoints of the critics themselves became clear.

As a result of the conference, Charles McKean of the Royal Incorporation of Architects in Scotland doubted that radical reconstruction could be classed as "restoration".[81] The Association of Conservation Officers expressed distress at the "inadequate understanding of traditional building construction" it was felt that several restorer-speakers displayed. Some architects chaffed at the work of other architects (or those who used no architects). And while those influenced by S.P.A.B. dogma argued against the dishonesty of "a built-in patina of age" in reconstructed work, others trained in the context-based ethos of modern conservation were concerned at the lack of sympathy of obvious modern interventions.

All in all, castle restoration was subjected to the sort of harsh (and sometimes justified) scrutiny rarely lavished on any other type of restored building. Ultimately, the most extreme view to surface was the archaeology-based standpoint that ruins should not be restored (for re-occupation) at all. While this view may tend to ignore any possible value for the future in the nature of restorations themselves, it accords well with the S.P.A.B. philosophy.

Castle restoration is unlikely to be stopped in its tracks while it remains the only viable solution for decaying structures where there is simply too much at risk of being lost. Seen as but the most recent manifestation of revivalism, as much as of restoration, substantially rebuilt structures of the quality of Aiket are easily capable of being appreciated in their own terms as the

Aiket - as reconstructed in the 18th century.

latest rendition of an auld (if somewhat re-written) song.

The charge of "faking" the past might be avoided by the simple and almost invisible incorporation of a "thin red line" of tiles between old and new; such was certainly practised by Robert Weir Schultz in his 1898 restoration of Wester Kames on Bute[82]. But conservation philosophies indeed weave a tangled web and Historic Scotland (which surely ought to preserve our heritage from the worst excesses of the less discriminating restorer) has of late argued the case for rebuilding faced in stone (rather than in concrete block or brick) under harl, so that old and new cannot be distinguished by visual inspection alone. But in fairness, Historic Scotland have never grant-aided fanciful restorations. Instead, they have concentrated on assisting cases where the original form of the building is understood and where original planning and other features can be reinstated, consolidating a heritage which has come down to us far less unaltered than domestic buildings of similar age in England.

Aiket - substantially reconstructed in the 20th century.

Sci-fi Scots Baronial?

As long ago as 1949, Compton MacKenzie had envisaged a modern Scottish Baronial style in his farce "Hunting the Fairies". The new and entirely fictional Keep of Knocknacolly exhibited a split-personality, resembling the Tower of London on one side and the Crystal Palace on the other. "Still, that young architect from Glasgow had made a good job of it, and there was no doubt that Dutton's [modernist and unhistoricist] cement cheese in Glenbore looked pretty second-rate after the Keep of Knocknacolly".

It may seem surprising that over almost half a century, no-one appears to have derived a modern Scots Baronial idiom using modern materials and modern design. Such an approach would certainly provide a solution to the dilemma of with what degree of "authenticity" to "mock-up" the past. It might also free revivalism in an exciting way from the constraints of castle-restoration and castle-rebuilding. There might also seem to be a social justification for such a bold move: increasingly, those attracted to castle restoration have been "middle class" rather than landed-gentry. Few own land beyond the immediate policies of their historic home. With an eye to the future, might not the partial democratization of "Old Scots" restorations represent new possibilities for the future?

There are, of course, good reasons why it might not. In many ways, castle-restoration and reconstruction has been a refuge from the "unromantic 20th century". Most importantly, the experience of the Thirties seemed to suggest that, freed from the texture and weathering qualities of traditional materials and the solidity of traditional construction, there would be little left with which to forge a new idiom which would be recognisably Scottish and Baronial.

On the other hand, Charles McKean has recently argued, even in the case of rebuilding ruins, for "a contemporary building that respects the ancient structure upon which it is set, but aspires, in contemporary plans and living forms, to communicate the ethos of what is attractive about the past without necessarily trying to fake it up...Given a creative designer, it is surely not impossible that we might see sitting upon its harled plinth a billowing glass superstructure spikily penetrating the clouds, rather than our tentative reconstructed skylines with their constipated dormers and hesitant cornices".

Pointing out that had they been alive today, the designers of the superstructures of the Palace of Bog o' Gight and the Palace of Balvenie would be unlikely to use anything other than contemporary materials, McKean continues:-

"*Ou sont les neiges d'antan?* Give me a castle: break out the contemporary architects: where are the Paolozzis of the skyline; where are the Goudies or Blackadders for mural paintings; where the Mores for the tapestries; where the Ian Hamilton Finlays for the armorial panels and the motifs? Where, in short, is the truly contemporary Scots culture as native, as European and as vigorous - but above all as logical and as intellectual - as that of our forefathers?"[83]

McKean's eloquent outburst may have been at least partly prompted by acquaintance with a young architect called Crichton Wood who is currently realising an ambition to attempt just such a thing at Castle Dhu near West Linton in the Borders. If Wood's plan - necessarily limited by budgetary constraints - is ever implemented, Castle Dhu will rise upwards on a splayed L-plan towards culmination in a glass bartizan. If client and architect succeed, they may point to a new affordable idiom beyond the long shadow of Arts & Crafts taste. But the pitfalls are hinted at by the split-personality of Compton MacKenzie's Knocknacolly. To go too far one way may make the new flamboyance seem incongruous; too far the other may loosen reference to the past. Only time and opportunity will tell.

Castle Dhu - model (Crichton Wood).

Osbert Lancaster's parody.

Skipness - interior of hall (Joanna Gordon).

Non-indigenous but characteristic.

Conclusion: a rather stale music hall joke?

"I am now convinced", wrote A.G.MacDonnell in 1937, "that Scotsmen must decide in the near future whether they wish to be citizens of a free country or citizens of a rather stale music hall joke".[84] As a major accoutrement of lairdship, Scots Baronial architecture might well have seemed by the Thirties to be suspiciously like another prop in the Harry Lauderesque wardrobe of self parody which Scotland would be best without.

Such a view certainly has much to support it. High Victorian Scots Baronial had no basis in any serious theory or belief, and the Arts & Crafts influenced Old Scots which succeeded it could claim little more than the justification of social and national context and greater identification with the "spirit" of old Scottish buildings. The philosophical credentials of the style were akin to the novels of Sir Walter Scott: historic fiction rather than fact. Its "nationalism" was generally that of the "quiet country member, who comes down to this old-world abode only for the shooting, and, on changing certain of his habiliments for the occasion, complains of taking cold in the knees".[85] Its political symbolism may have been "noble by association with ideas of power", but that power was "of an obsolete order".[86] The style might therefore be easily presented as the perfect stuff of Scots Victorian and Edwardian romance, with no significance other than pride in tradition and social class.

Despite the appeal of the style to the incoming English laird, it was scarcely built outside Scotland (with the sole exception of the protestant areas of Ireland, where identification with the early protestant settlers carried special connotations not found in Scotland). While English Tudor or Elizabethan manor-house styles became a legitimate British style, Scots Baronial remained localised within Scotland. By the Edwardian period, within Scotland, new mansions in English manorial idioms easily outnumbered those in Scottish styles. Even Mackintosh's houses absorbed to a considerable degree the influence of English Arts & Crafts revivalism. To architectural historian Henry Russel-Hitchcock, High Victorian Scots Baronial was merely a sub-category "somewhere between the Edwardian Castellated and the irregular Jacobethan Manorial",[87] both (of course) English styles.

While Compton MacKenzie poked fun at High Victorian interior decoration in general in his description of imaginary Kilwhillie House,[88] Osbert Lancaster drew attention to the more self consciously Scottish elements of Scots Baronial interior design. Although, in some senses, the Scots Baronial interior scarcely existed as a precise revival style, the general effect was sufficiently well recognised to permit gamey parody when conjuring up "these enormous necropolitan menageries stuffed full of stags and caribou, bears and tigers", portraits of "rank upon rank of grim-visaged, elaborately kilted forbears", and the obligatory splattering of "tartan, stags' heads and faithful representations of Highland cattle...".[89] In truth, it was not impossible to find a real interior which boasted amidst its decor the china out of which Dr Johnson drank his thirteen cups of tea at Raasay in 1772, the dirk of an ancestor who fell at Sherrifmuir, a drum used in the Crimea, and exotics such as bronze age weapons, spears from the armoury of the Citadel of Cairo, and some pieces of mosaic from the bath of the King of Delhi![90] At Dougarie on Arran, the exterior was covered "from top to bottom with stags' antlers...the hall and passages and stairs were panelled shoulder-high with deerskins, the stick racks were deer antlers, so were the door knobs...".[91] The drawing room had a window over the fireplace so that the drama of the hills could be appreciated by those warming themselves at the fire.

To earnest Modernists, however, it was not simply the tartanry of taste, the "Bloodsports Baronial"[92] trophies, or the High Victorian "Balmorality" which had become unacceptable: Scots Baronial, from Burn to Lorimer, was simply irrelevant to the pressing needs of society and the direction of architecture. Thomas Howarth freely concluded that although Lorimer's work was often "delightful and charming", his "positive contribution to architectural development is questionable".[93] Beyond Lorimer, the restoration of castles in recent years has been considered an irrelevance in a different sense, turning archaeology and history into the playthings of "instant lairds". Charles McKean in particular has expressed concern over lack of sympathy for, and understanding of, historic Scots buildings and has referred to "the Scottish preoccupation with its invented, misconceived and misunderstood past".

Yet, in spite of all of this, Scots Baronial is worthy of serious study and even praise. It was, first and foremost, part of a European movement of exploration of national identity which saw Scotland as a land of historic romance and romantic history. If Scots Baronial occasionally veered towards absurdity, it more often embodied the subordination of historic precedent to contemporary requirements. It was characterised by greater compositional drama than was the case with many of its continental equivalents. While the baronial idiom of David Bryce and his followers looms large, there were and are a variety of approaches which have exercised their varied appeal down to the present day. While some manifestations of the style could on occasion be too colourful for the observer not to enjoy the thrill of their notoriety, the exaggerated emblems of Scottishness (rather than symbols of real national life) which characterised the Revival as a whole might seem significant as evidence of, and compensation for, a threatened culture.

The West of Scotland - particularly the undeniably romantic West Highlands - is a particularly significant area of study, not simply because of the interest or even variety of the individual houses, but because of an underlying culture which associated such houses with such a setting and as the appropriate environment for highland lairdship. It is this in particular which may help to explain the concentration of "antiquarian" houses in Argyll. In 1772, James Boswell was moved to "resolute feudal enthusiasm"[94] while on his tour to the Hebrides with Dr Johnson. The 3rd Duke of Argyll took seriously "his feudal status and responsibilities. As soon as the new castle [at Inveraray] was roofed over, he began successful proceedings against the MacAlistair captains of Tarbert Castle for failing to maintain that ruined towerhouse...".[95] Subsequently, a number of new Campbell houses wisely boasted crenellations clamped to their wallheads!

In Argyll also, there are signs that "resolute feudal

"Bloodsports Baronial"
at Braemore in Ross-shire (C. Boyd).

Inverawe - interior.

Inverawe - interior.

*Kilted client - John MacRae
Gilstrap of Ballimore and Eilean Donan:
ancient lineage, new money and a Gaelic
speaking mother.*

enthusiasm" was alive and well, with a culture of its own, well into the 19th century. Around 1800, it was not unknown, though possibly not usual, for Argyll gentlemen to adopt the kilt for normal attire.[96] By the 1860s, Argyll backwoods gentry of the old, Campbell descent might wear the kilt as a matter of course. John Francis Campbell of the Islay family did so, and took trouble to collect folktales while they were still in circulation. His "tutor and nurse" had been the family piper. John Campbell of Kilberry robustly pursued his pastimes of shooting and highland dancing: he was clearly not alone in the vigour with which he dedicated himself to the latter, as revealed by his diaries: in one by no means untypical entry,[97] he noted that Campbell of Ormsary and Mrs & Miss Campbell of Dunmore visited in the afternoon "and we danced like smoke all night to Hewie's Pipes..". All night, in John Campbell's terms, generally meant literally until dawn. He and his dancing partners from Dunmore owned convincingly "antiquarian" houses, and the MacDonald-Moretons who commissioned Largie Castle - most "antiquarian" of all the Argyll mansions of the mid-century - were socially familiar with the families of Kilberry and Dunmore.

It is surely not fanciful to see in the enthusiasms of lairds such as John Campbell of Kilberry a genuine, 19th century Scots Baronial culture. After a period as a soldier in India, he was to succeed as laird and return to "Bryce" his family seat with a wing by Peddie & Kinnear, and to bedeck the main hall with tiger skins, heads of antelope and prize winning cattle as trophies, and much else besides...

As late as the decades after the Second World War, one could still glimpse kenspeckle Argyll gentry in faded tartan, a uniform today reserved virtually only (and in pristine condition) for hoteliers and wedding parties. Perhaps the most conspicuous, grandly accoutred laird of relatively recent times was Duncan MacRae of Ballimore, "bearing himself with such antique bravura"[98] as he indulged his passion for drinking and providing whisky all over Cowal. This now legendary, colourful, roaring figure, more unlikely than anyone ever imagined by Compton MacKenzie, had raised his father's standard over Eilean Donan on its completion and, in later years, was a frequent visitor at the Glendaruel Hotel which supplied him with snacks of several cold, cooked grouse which he would carry away in his sporran.[99] But here, once more, our examination of baronial culture has ended in a kind of caricature, or at least in an extreme; no matter, for as Kerr has already told us of the architectural style, "to subdue is to weaken".

In the end, one must make one's own mind up about so rich and gamey a baronial dish. Perhaps the best assessment of the Scots Baronial Revival was made as long ago as 1967, when T.W.West summed up the work of David Bryce as "the architectural equivalent of Horatio MacCulloch's magnificently romantic landscapes".[100] He also pointed out that, at worst, Scots Baronial had its equivalent in the commercialised tartan of the Victorian age. From our own standpoint, we should be able to appreciate the considerable merits of its high points and view, with amused interest, its more "atmospheric" excesses.

NOTES TO TEXT

1. Sir John Stirling Maxwell, *Shrines and homes of Scotland*, 1937, p.206.
2. *Ibid.* p.203.
3. Frank Walker, unpublished lecture delivered at the Architectural Heritage Society of Scotland 1993 Strathclyde conference, *Scots Baronial*.
4. See: Ian G Lindsay & Mary Cosh, *Inveraray and the Dukes of Argyll*, 1973, pp. 35-106 and also: James Macaulay, *The Gothic Revival 1745-1845*, 1975, pp. 40-55.
5. David Walker, *William Burn* in: Jane Fawcett (ed.), *Seven Victorian architects*, 1976, pp. 20-21.
6. *See: Ibid.*, p. 10.
7. *Ibid.*, p. 22.
8. Henry-Russell Hitchcock, *Early Victorian architecture in Britain*, 1954, p. 248. "The essentially Jacobethan character of the main block is moderately 'Scotticized', as it were, by the stepped gables and the pepper-pot turrets on the corner pavilions." See also, David Walker, *op. cit.*, p.31.
9. Robert Kerr, *The gentleman's house*, 1864, 3rd ed. 1871, p. 378.
10. *Ibid.*, p. 378.
11. *Ibid.*, p. 450.
12. See: Michael C. Davis, *The castles and mansions of Ayrshire*, 1991, p.182.
13. James Macaulay, *The Gothic Revival 1745-1845*, 1979, p.336.
14. Michael C. Davis, op. cit., p.90.
15. The authorship of David Cousin for the Newark additions was not realized in 1991 when, in *The castles and mansions of Ayrshire* (*op. cit.*) I noted that the work there had some similarities with the work of W.H.Playfair. Rob Close, *Ayrshire and Arran: an illustrated architectural guide*, 1992, uncovered Cousin's authorship. From this starting point, Cousin's obituary in *The Edinburgh Courant*, Sept. 4th, 1878, revealed responsibility for the Maybole Castle additions, and the Kilhenzie restoration and additions of the same period may be attributed on stylistic grounds.
16. J.C.Loudon, *Cottage, farm, and villa architecture*, 1839, p.889.
17. It would be difficult to summarise the achievement of David Bryce without expressing obvious debt to: Valerie Fiddes & Alistair Rowan, *David Bryce 1803-1876*, 1976. Even to talk of Bryce's "ruthless exploitation" of his visual sources is to use words first coined by Alistair Rowan (p. 20).
18. *The Builder* obituary, quoted in: David Walker, *Master of the grand manner* in: *Country Life*, October 28, 1976, p. 1211.
19. Robert Billings, *The baronial and ecclesiastical antiquities of Scotland*, 4 vols. 1845-52.
20. Robert Kerr, *op. cit.*, p. 337.
21. Valerie Fiddes & Alistair Rowan, *op. oit.*, p.19.
22. Charles McKean, *Stirling and the Trossachs: an illustrated architectural guide*, 1985, p. 132.
23. Jack Sloan's excellent *Dalzell*, 1986, correctly points out that the retaining wall to the terraced garden is Billings' "most direct quote from Scottish Renaissance architecture", being based on the garden wall at Edzell.
24. Henry, Lord Cockburn, *Circuit journeys*, 1983 ed., pp. 124-5
25. I am grateful to David Walker for advising on the architectural evolution and probable dating of Dunmore.
26. Skipness was commissioned by a rich mother for her 21 year old son, Robert Chellas Graham, who was both an antiquary and interested in technological innovation. His sister apparently had the position of a proposed corner tower moved (to the position in which it was in fact built) in order to accord with her own ideas as an amateur architect. Robert's mother wanted to see her family transmigrate from Glaswegian mercantile status to Highland lairdship. She had the money to effect the change. [Information courtesy of Joanna Gordon.]
27. Angus Henderson, *Kildalton House* in: *The Scottish Field*, June 1916, p. 287, attributes the design of the house to its owner, John Ramsay, "assisted by the late Mr Charles Morrison of Islay and other friends."
28. Charles Kinnear was a former Bryce pupil.
29. Valerie Fiddes & Alistair Rowan, *op. cit.*, p.16.
30. *Gruline House* (anon.) in: *The Scots Pictorial*, May 29, 1920, p620.
31. Dated on the basis of the valuation rolls (courtesy of Murdo MacDonald, Argyll & Bute District Archivist), and OS maps. The later dating in RCAHMS *Argyll*, Vol. 7, 1992, p.92 is clearly in error. The family tradition of the Fletchers of Dunans is that an Edinburgh architect called Carr or Kerr was responsible: this was almost certainly Andrew Kerr, an Office of Works architect who carried out some work in a baronial vein at Lodge Journeymen Masons in

Blackfriars Street in Edinburgh and who restored Doune for the Earl of Moray and Roslin Chapel for the Earl of Rosslyn. There is a stronger similarity with the baronial work of J. Anderson Hamilton at 50-58 Bernard Street (1864) in Leith. Was Kerr by any chance working with Hamilton in 1864?
32. The description "pantomime gunloops" is almost certainly a McKean*ism*.
33. Robert Kerr, *op. cit.*, p. 449.
34. Hermann Muthesius, *The English house*, 1987 English edition of 1908-11 2nd ed., p.62.
35. Gavin Stamp, unpublished introductory remarks to the Architectural Heritage Society of Scotland 1993 Strathclyde conference, *Scots Baronial*.
36. Hermann Muthesius, *op. cit.*, p.62.
37. *Ibid.*
38. The title of Sam McKinstry's lecture at the Architectural Heritage Society of Scotland 1993 Strathclyde conference, *Scots Baronial*. Charles McKean, in: *Architectural contributions to Scottish Society since 1840*, 1990, p.17, referred to the Second revival. By 1995, McKean was writing of "the third Scottish architectural revival, of which Charles Rennie Mackintosh was such a significant part" (*Charles Rennie Mackintosh Society Newsletter No.67*, Summer 1995, p.11).
39. Gavin Stamp, *Stamp album* in: *The Herald*, Saturday 30th October 1993. David Wal;ker suggests J.M.Wardrop's Kinnardy Castle as the precursor of this school of design.
40. Sir John Stirling-Maxwell, *op. cit.*, p.205.
41. For further information on Balnowlart, Southwood and Silverglades, see: Michael C. Davis, *Castles and mansions of Ayrshire*, 1991, and: *Millionaireshire mansions* in: *The Age of Mackintosh* (ed. John Lowry), 1992.
42. For information on T.A. Millar's houses, see: *The late Mr Andrew Millar* in *Quarterly of the Incorporation of Architects in Scotland*, 1922, pp.8-11.
43. Charles McKean, *op.cit.*, p.137.
44. For further discussion of Killean, Kintyre, see: David Walker, *The domestic designs of Sir John James Burnet* in *Scottish country houses 1600-1914*, ed. Ian Gow and Alistair Rowan, 1995, pp. 299-300.
45. Gavin Stamp, *Stamp album* in: *The Herald*, Saturday 30th October 1993.
46. Gavin Stamp, unpublished introductory remarks to The Architectural heritage Society of Scotland 1993 Strathclyde conference, *Scots Baronial*.
47. The Auchenbothie Gate Lodge scheme is reproduced in: Pamela Robertson, *C.R.Mackintosh architecture drawings*, Hunterian Art Gallery, 1990 Glasgow University Exhibition Catalogue p.25.
48. C.R.Mackintosh, quoted in: Pamela Robertson, *Charles Rennie Mackintosh, the architectural papers*, 1990, p.188.
49. For discussion of the country houses of J.K.Hunter, see: Michael C. Davis, *The castles and mansions of Ayrshire*, 1991, pp.110-111.
50. James Macaulay, *Hill House*, 1994, p.13.
51. Charles Rennie Mackintosh, *Untitled paper on architecture* in: *Charles Rennie Mackintosh: the architectural papers*, ed. P. Robertson, 1990, p.188, and quoted in: James Macaulay, *Hill House*, 1994, p13.
52. Simon Green, *William Leiper's houses in Helensburgh* in: *The Age of Mackintosh*, ed. John Lowry, 1992, p.35.
53. Frank Arneil Walker, *North Clyde Estuary: an illustrated architectural guide*, 1992, p.89.
54. *Men who build* in: *The Builder's Journal and Architectural Record*, Jan. 12th 1989, p.487.
55. *Glasgow at a glance*, ed. A.M. Doak & Andrew McLaren Young, 1965 & 1977, item 166.
56. Sir John Stirling-Maxwell, *op. cit.*, p.206.
57. William Hunter McNab, *William Leiper, R.S.A., J.P.* in: *The Journal of the Royal Institute of British Architects*, 26th Aug.1916, p.304.
58. *Ballimore, Argyllshire*, (anon.) in: *The Scots Pictorial*, Nov. 1st 1919.
59. E.g. at Chateau Josselyn, restored by a disciple of Violet-le-Duc, M. de la Morandiere, from 1866 and completed in the late 19th century by M. Henri Lafargne.
60. After work had begun the plans were altered to permit another storey, presumably the attic. Information from *The Oban Times* Feb. 12th 1906, courtesy of Murdo MacDonald, Argyll & Bute District Archivist.
61. David Walker, *The Honeymans* in: *Charles Rennie Mackintosh Society Newsletter No. 64*, Spring 1994, p.8.
62. Precisely this progression has been noted by Peter Savage, *Lorimer and the Edinburgh craft designers*, 1980, p.108.

63. John MacRae, *Eilean Donan Castle*, 1978 (official guide book), p.4.
64. Peter Savage, *op. cit.*, p.109.
65. Charles McKean, *Introduction* to: J.M. Fladman et al., *Tomorrow's architectural heritage; landscape and buildings in the countryside*, p.13. In fairness to McKean, one should add that his critique of Lorimer is capable of greater subtelty than this single quote might imply. He stresses that while Lorimer designed "with his eyes", Mackintosh "intuitively came to understand how they [old Scottish buildings] could be a model for contemporary architecture...Lorimer's proportions are such that you never saw in old Scottish buildings whereas Mackintosh's proportions almost are".
66. Hermann Muthesius, *op. cit.*, p.62.
67. Christopher Hussey, *op. cit.*, p.206.
68. Sir John Stirling-Maxwell, *op. cit.*, p.206.
69. *Ibid.*
70. Christopher Hussey, *op. cit.*, p.69.
71. Peter Savage, *Lorimer and the Edinburgh craft designers*, 1980, p.60.
72. Elaine Wheeler/The Formakin Trust, *Formakin; a short history* (undated but c.1990). In this short but well researched booklet, Wheeler also quotes a telegram from Holms to Lorimer, indicating the extent of the client's interest in minute detail: "Did not like windows at Formakin supposed to be Aberdour, find you have mucked them up, don't want imaginings of a heated brain, it's Aberdour I want and Aberdour I shall have".
73. Sir John Stirling-Maxwell, quoted in: Charles McKean, *The Scottish Thirties*, 1987, p.57.
74. Ian G. Lindsay, *Quarterly of the Incorporation of Architects in Scotland*, no.52, 1936, quoted in: Charles McKean, *The Scottish Thirties*, 1987, p.55.
75. Robert Hurd, *Scotland*, 1938, p.21, quoted in: Charles McKean, *The Scottish Thirties*, 1987, p.55.
76. Thanks to the war, Keil Hotel did not open until 1947.
77. Gerald Laing, *Kinkell, the reconstruction of a Scottish castle*, 2nd ed., 1984, p.6.
78. "So far I've been allowed to do a few 14th century interiors at a castle near Aberdour", Simon Fleming in *The Herald: Scotland's Houses Supplement*, Dec. 7th 1994, p.22.
79. Harriet Richardson, *Lorimer's castle restorations* in: *The age of Mackintosh, op. cit.*, p.70.
80. In 1897, in a paper to The Edinburgh Architectural Association, Lorimer declared that "it is quite impossible to restore an old gothic building. You can mend it. You can keep it in repair and prevent it from falling down but to restore it is, and always will be, absolutely impossible" (see: Harriet Richardson, *op. cit.*). Such S.P.A.B. piety, echoing Morris, Ruskin and Lethaby, may seem surprising in view of Lorimer's later work, but it is really only a matter of semantics. The word "restoration", then associated with a more vandalistic approach, had pejorative overtones in the 1890s among the architecturally aware. Lord Bute had "a dislike of the word 'restoration', as applied to ancient edifices which were, and still are, so often spoiled in the process" (Fr. Hunter Blair, quoted in: Gavin Stamp, *Robert Weir Schultz and his work for the Marquesses of Bute*, 1981, p.43). Yet, Bute had himself in 1897 initiated a rebuilding of Wester Kames on Bute to the designs of Robert Weir Schultz, "based on no concrete evidence of its original appearance other than comparison with similar buildings" (Gavin Stamp, , *Ibid.*, p.43). A thin red line of tiles divided the 17th century base from the new reconstruction. "Reconstruction" was indeed the term favoured by Schultz in reference to his work at Brunton House at Falkland in Fife (Gavin Stamp, *Ibid.*, pp.31-32). Stamp comments that "Schultz could not have used the pejorative term 'restoration' ".
81. *Chambers 20th century dictionary*, 1983 edition, not only defines "restoration" as bringing back "to a (supposed) former state", but also as "rennovations and reconstruction (sometimes little differing from destruction)".
82. Gavin Stamp, *Robert Weir Schultz and his work for the Marquesses of Bute*, 1981, p.43.
83. Charles McKean, *Restoring castles*, 1992 (unpublished paper).
84. A.G. MacDonell, *My Scotland*, 1937.
85. Robert Kerr, *op.cit.*, p.337.
86. *Ibid.*, p.337.
87. Henry Russel-Hitchcock, *Early Victorian architecture in Britain*, Vol. 1, p.246.
88. "...the interior had been packed as only mid-Victorians knew how to pack their houses with heavy furniture, bad pictures, ugly hangings and preposterous bric-a-brac...the drawing room...looked like the shop of an antique dealer in Brompton Road".
89. Osbert Lancaster, *Homes sweet homes*, 1938, p.40.
90. Just such a collection was to be found at Ballimore House, Argyll, in 1919. What remains of it is now at Eilean Donan.
91. Lady Jean Fforde, *Castles in the air*, 1982, p.106.
92. "Bloodsports Baronial" was coined by Ian Gow in his lecture, *The problem of the Scottish Baronial interior*, at The Architectural Heritage Society of Scotland 1993 Strathclyde Conference, *Scots Baronial*. The lecture may soon be published.
93. Thomas Howarth, *Charles Rennie Mackintosh and the Modern Movement*, 1977, pp.93-94.
94. James Boswell, *The journal of a tour to the Hebrides with Samuel Johnson*, 1785 (1958 Everyman's Library edition, p.149-50).
95. RCAHMS, *Argyll, Vol. 7*, pp.26, 29 & 538.
96. In 1799, George Malcolm, a wealthy member of a Mid Argyll family rising to riches through Jamaican estates, had his attacks of fever blamed upon his wearing the kilt on a trip to Inverness! [Poltalloch Papers, Argyll & Bute District Archives].
97. John Campbell of Kilberry, *Diaries 1861-62* (in the care of the Argyll & Bute District Council Archivist).
98. Iain Hamilton & Ann Thomas, *The Kerry Kyle*, 1980, p.26.
99. Information courtesy of Louise Watson.
100. T.W. West, *A history of architecture in Scotland*, 1976, p.172.

A NOTE ON GARDENS

The setting for the house - the garden and policies of the Scots Baronial mansion - rarely differed from that laid out around a Scottish country house in a different style. The response was, on the whole, to contemporary requirements and tastes, and to the potential of the site, rather than to history.

However, since castle styles were early linked with a rugged or highland landscape, a woodland garden with its particularly West Coast flavour of exotic rhododendrons was the inevitable setting of many a Scots Baronial pile outwith the rolling pastures of Ayrshire and the lowland counties. Stonefield Castle, a romantic house in an equally romantic setting above Loch Fyne, is noteworthy in this respect. There, an important collection of rhododendrons was developed from seed collected by Sir Joseph Hooker around 1850, and the many walks laid out provided a model for future West Coast gardens.

Robert Billings and his client at Dalzell, John Hamilton, made an early attempt to revive a Scots Renaissance garden from 1857. Long described as "Italian", this terraced garden has been reassessed by Jack Sloan (*Dalzell*, 1986, pp.8-10) who points out that its topiary pyramids, globes and obelisks and its clipped box parterre were doubtless influenced by the fabulous Scots Renaissance garden at nearby Barncluith .

Billings and his client's noble effort was scarcely taken up until the time of Robert Lorimer. Lorimer's work to establish an enclosed garden at Earlshall, immediately adjacent to the house, clearly took inspiration from the great Old Scots gardens elsewhere in the East of Scotland, notably Pitmedden and Edzell; but the concept was scarcely developed in the great West Coast mansions despite the appearance at Rowallan and Formakin of ogee roofed garden pavilions. Even John Holms' formal garden, laid out by Lorimer at Formakin, had a great contemporary emphasis on wide borders and open lawns. He was probably too much a plant-collector and romantic to surrender unconditionally to the mathematical certainties of box parterres.

The work of Thomas Mawson, an English landscape architect, was given a good airing in Scotland around the turn of the century and, although he did not alter his style to overtly express Scottish sentiment, he tended to respond extremely well to the potential offered by the topography. At Ballimore he created probably his most impressive Scottish garden, sculpting a stream in a ditch into a gurgling highland burn, splashing down to the sea through ponds, miniature waterfalls and rocky pools. Above it and its glen, he surrounded the house (remodelled by William Leiper) with formal lawns, topiary walks, elaborate bedding and a great terrace overlooking the burn and exotic rhododendrons. Though it has suffered years of neglect, its features are still recognisable.

Recently, splendid attempts have been made to restore the Barncluith gardens, and castle restorers have created a number of new gardens of variable quality and size, notably well designed at Aiket and (on a more constricted site) at Castle Leven. Probably thanks to the relatively limited survival (or existence) of early pleasure gardens, the idea of a garden based on historic Scottish precedent has received little expression over the years.

ERRATA

Page 31 - The drawing room furnishings illustrated are of course later.
Page 38 - Lorimer moved from Bodley's office by 1891 not 1901.